REWRITING SECRETS
FOR SCREENWRITERS

ALSO BY TOM LAZARUS

Secrets of Film Writing

*RE*WRITING SECRETS FOR SCREENWRITERS

Seven Strategies to Improve and Sell Your Work

Tom Lazarus

ST. MARTIN'S GRIFFIN
NEW YORK

www.stmartins.com

Library of Congress Cataloging-in-Publication Data

Lazarus, Tom.
    Rewriting secrets for screenwriters : seven strategies to improve and sell your work / Tom Lazarus.—1st St. Martin's Griffin ed.
        p. cm.
    ISBN 0-312-33831-7
    EAN 978-0-312-33831-2
    1. Motion picture authorship.   2. Motion picture plays—Editing.   I. Title.

PN1996.L379 2006
808.2'3—dc22

                                                                        2005044457

First Edition: April 2006

10   9   8   7   6   5   4   3   2   1

To Stevie:

Before I met her, whenever I wrote a script with another writer, my characters would invariably kill off their characters. Now when I collaborate, my characters only wound the other writer's characters.

I can thank Stevie for that progress.

CONTENTS

FOREWORD BY SCOTT FRANK

Scott's credits include *Minority Report* and *Get Shorty*, as well as too-numerous-to-mention un-credited rewrites on many of Hollywood's biggest studio releases.

There is nothing worse than reading a half-baked screenplay. There is nothing more frustrating than reading a piece of work (or even worse, actually *seeing* it on screen) where no one has bothered to answer even the most basic questions, let alone the more difficult ones.

First drafts are all about making mistakes. They are by definition full of blind alleys and, if we're lucky, happy accidents. Gradually we shape (will) our script into a story that makes some degree of sense; a story that has a beginning, a middle, and an end, all limning the vaguest suggestion of a movie.

For many new writers, this is the end of the process. After all, the "document" *looks* like a completed script. And, as any serious writer will tell you, it's so damn hard to finish a screenplay—the process so fraught with agony and indecision—that we rarely want to go back and revisit the pain once we've completed the task.

But the truth is, that's where all the really great work begins.

The many successive drafts, then, become the true honing of the story. We discover character not in the broad sense but through nuance that can only come from further and deeper exploration. The writer who avoids this opportunity to discover is as misguided as the portrait painter who only looks once at his subject before painting it. Think of all that he misses! It is only through many layers of paint that true complexity can be uncovered.

We're often thwarted by our own expectations. We expect that once we type "Fade Out" or "The End," we're finished. Later we expect that once our film gets green lit we're done. Or once the film is in the can, we're finished. We're *never* done and we should never expect to be. We should expect to be constantly rewriting our material. We should expect the process of uncovering those layers, of getting our story to work on several levels at once, to go on forever. In fact, standing in the back of the theater, we should expect to be wistfully rewriting scenes as they play out in front of an actual audience.

This way, when we are either forced to return to our material or simply succumb to our own gnawing guilt, we're not really surprised. Just maybe a little disappointed that, yet again, we weren't provided with that once-in-a-lifetime gift from God, that blessed period of time when an artist finds himself or herself breathlessly channeling an idea whole cloth onto the page or canvas. It gives us something to look forward to.

In the meantime, you have Tom Lazarus to help you cope with your disappointment and your reluctance and your thwarted expectations. Tom, the first "real" screenwriter I ever met, some twenty-two years ago, is a master of making the complex appear simple without ever lulling one into a false sense of competence through either reductive formula or glib strategies.

It's all about a story well told. It's about not shrinking away from the often long and difficult task of discovery. The truth is, that very task is often the most fun, the most exhilarating part of writing. There is nothing more addictive than spending your days awake, yet dreaming, walking through your own fantasy.

Off you go.

For Tom Lazarus's interview with Scott Frank, visit http://tomlazarus.com.

INTRODUCTION

My first book, *Secrets of Film Writing,* taught me a lot of things. One, it was fun to write. Two, it put me in contact with a lot of screenwriters—all kinds of writers, actually—and it was wonderful to get their appreciative reactions to the ideas and war stories in the book. It was clear by their comments they weren't looking to learn about the influence of early French cinema on contemporary story structure; they wanted—and got—practical, from-the-trenches straight talk about screenwriting and the realities of the up-and-down, ultimately wonderful life of a screenwriter. The common theme among the writers who e-mailed me was rewriting. They asked lots of questions about rewriting. Lots and lots of questions about rewriting.

The apparent lack of a rewriting resource for screenwriters, plus the desire to make some money, prompted me to write *Rewriting Secrets for Screenwriters.* Bear with me, if you would, about the title. I'm trying to build a franchise here. You know: *Secrets of Writing for Television, Secrets of Writing Thank-You Notes,* and *Secrets of Writing Books with the Word "Secrets" in the Title.*

Let's start at the beginning. **The cliché "writing is rewriting" is the absolute truth.**

After all the preparation for writing: scene lists, beat sheets, three-by-five cards, whatever your process is, this first rough draft is terrific fun to write, to just race through the idea, following your storytelling instincts, going with the flow, letting everything hang out. The first rough draft is really just the blocking out of the script. It's loose. It's rough. It's creative. I take chances. I don't censor anything. **It's the blueprint for a screenplay.** It's then the hard work, the real writing, begins. It's called *rewriting*.

Let's get one thing straight: *I love rewriting.* Why? Because it's so damned satisfying.

Rewriting maximizes ideas.

Rewriting makes the story rounder and richer.

Rewriting brings rough-draft scene descriptions to life.

Rewriting raises characters from cardboard to memorable and castable.

Rewriting evolves the important scenes from workmanlike to unforgettable.

Rewriting allows writing to mature, to season, to be perfected.

Rewriting facilitates making connections and resonances that deepen the screenplay.

Rewriting makes your writing better.

The bottom line: Rewriting helps you evolve your screenplays to the rich, full page-turners that are necessary to be viable in today's incredibly competitive marketplace.

In *Rewriting Secrets for Screenwriters,* in addition to introducing a seven-part Strategy for Rewriting, and writing about the many different kinds of rewriting, I share the specifics of actual examples of rewriting, giving you models of rewriting to learn from. You'll be able take this information and apply it to your own work. There are also some hair-raising rewriting war stories.

I guarantee if you do all the things I write about in this book, you'll sell your screenplay, make millions, and retire to get fat and happy.

Well, maybe not.

But, one thing is certain: Your screenplays will get better, a lot better.

Keep writing.

Tom Lazarus
http://tomlazarus.com

RE WRITING SECRETS

FOR SCREENWRITERS

One

WHY GREAT FILMS ARE GREAT

GONE WITH THE WIND

BASED ON MARGARET MITCHELL'S EPIC NOVEL, SYDNEY Howard's first-draft screenplay for *Gone with the Wind* was an excessive four hundred pages long. Over the next two and half years, the producer, the legendary David O. Selznick, hired writers Jo Swerling, Oliver H. P. Garrett, F. Scott Fitzgerald, John Van Druten, and Charles MacArthur to do rewrites before *Gone with the Wind* went into production. George Cukor started shooting, but was fired as director two weeks later. He was replaced by Victor Fleming, who refused to film a single scene until he had a realistic shooting script, prompting even more rewrites by Ben Hecht. Still unsatisfied, Selznick brought back Sydney Howard's screenplay and Ben Hecht rewrote *that*.

Right before production, Sydney Howard himself was brought back to do some additional writing. Six writers. Countless rewrites.

THE WIZARD OF OZ

The first of a dozen screenwriters consulted on *The Wizard of Oz* was Irving Brecher. Herman J. Mankiewicz wrote the official first draft, which was rejected by MGM. Then, Ogden Nash did a rewrite as did playwright Knoll Langley, who continued on the project for three months and wrote many, many drafts. Langley's rewrite was ultimately unfilmable and the producers brought in another writer, Samuel Hoffenstein, who only worked for a few days. Langley continued rewriting and finished the "shooting script." Producers Mervyn LeRoy and Arthur Freed brought in the veteran writing team of Florence Ryerson and Edgar Allan Woolf to do a rewrite, but it was still not considered right by the studio and they brought Langley back. He rewrote Woolf and Ryerson. Edgar "Yip" Harburg, who had worked on the score, was also brought in to do some rewriting. Writers Jack Mintz and Sid Silvers did even more rewriting. When Victor Fleming was brought in as director, he had writer John Lee Mahin hired to do some final rewriting before they started shooting.

CITIZEN KANE

Arguably the greatest film of all time was a collaboration between Orson Welles and Herman J. Mankiewicz. Mankiewicz wrote an excessive 250-page first draft. (Screenplays today run from 95 to 135 pages. It better be good if it's 135 pages.) Changes were made in that script and a second draft was completed. Mankiewicz left the project, but rewrites continued under the supervision of John Houseman. A writer named Amalia Kent was the next writer to do a rewrite, then Welles worked on the rewrite after her. Welles rewrote a hundred seventy pages and deleted more than seventy-five pages. The picture was budgeted . . . way over budget. Welles was forced to do even more rewrites. After that, Mankiewicz was brought back onto the project and generated three new rewrites. Another rewrite was generated for the Hays office, a self-regulating standards and practices organization set up by the motion picture industry. Finally they had an official shooting script.

CASABLANCA

The film classic *Casablanca* began its life as a play by author Murray Burnett. Hal Wallis, the producer of the film, brought in his brother-in-law, Wally Kline, and his writing partner, Aeneas Mac-Kenzie, to do work on the script. They worked for seven weeks. Even before they finished, Wallis was talking with twins Julius and Philip Epstein about the script. They wrote and rewrote until they completed the "final" script. Another writer, Casey Robinson, was hired and worked for three weeks doing rewrites. Still unsatisfied, Wallis brought in Howard Koch to rewrite the first part of the script.

Lenore Coffee also worked on the script for a week. It turned out the Epsteins were rewriting the second part of the script and Howard Koch was rewriting the Epsteins' first act. Ultimately, seven writers worked on *Casablanca*.

SO, WHAT DOES ALL THIS MEAN?

It indicates to me that a great film from a great screenplay takes lots of work, great creativity, and most of all *rewriting*. I know this isn't a surprise. After all, this is a book about rewriting.

When I first started reading screenplays, I thought that writers wrote what I was reading out of the chute. That it just came out onto the page perfectly the first time. That's what a right writer was.

I didn't know about rewrites.

I didn't know about restructuring.

I didn't know about working scenes to make them better.

I didn't know about developing threads and arcs and subplots and subtext. Hello?

It's clear to me now that it takes time and many drafts to make a script great. It's clear to me now that the cliché "A horse designed by committee is a camel" isn't true at all. Sometimes, a horse designed by committee is a triple-crown winner.

TWO

A STRATEGY FOR REWRITING

NORMALLY, I'M A PROPONENT OF WRITING FROM THE GUT AND trusting your storytelling instincts, so it's a little odd for me to propose a formalized Strategy for Rewriting. What I'm really up to is proposing a new and different way to think about rewriting. The key, of course, is to *think about rewriting*. It all starts there.

You know the famous shot in *The Matrix* where multiple cameras take 360 degrees of photographs of Keanu Reeves and when they meld them together in the film we, amazingly, wheel around him showing every angle of him moving through the air? That's how I visualize the process of rewriting.

Keanu Reeves is your screenplay. The Strategy for Rewriting is the cameras viewing Keanu from all sides.

This Strategy for Rewriting takes a 360-degree look at your screenplay.

This Strategy for Rewriting is composed of *seven separate minirewrites*—seven secrets, if you will—each one targeting a different facet of the screenplay.

The Strategy for Rewriting allows you to isolate characteristics of your writing so you can—divorced of story—be more objective about them.

Objectivity about your writing leads, inevitably, to improvement.

After you've rewritten a couple of screenplays using the Strategy for Rewriting, you'll see how it dramatically raises the level of your writing and your screenplays.

Secret #1:
Gaining New Perspectives

Most of us find it's easier to critique someone else's screenplay than our own. It's one of the truisms of screenwriting. The reason? We have a clear perspective on their work. We haven't toiled over each word, spent weeks and months perfecting it. We see it fresh.

The key to rewriting your screenplay is to be able to *step away from it* to get into a position where you can see the different aspects of your screenplay anew. It's important with any rewrite, but particularly when you are rewriting your own screenplay.

After you've finished your rough draft, put it down. Do something else. Cleaning your workspace is always good. Get that long-needed haircut. Clean your keyboard—mine always has a disgusting mix of cookie crumbs, salt, dust, unidentifiable herbal material, and dirt. Organize your files. Repot some plants. Read some good, inspiring fiction. Go into rehab. Anything that gets you out of your head and shakes up your brain cells so you can be fresh when you return to your screenplay. It could be a couple of days. It could be a week.

When I return to my screenplay, **the first thing I do is create a scene list.** The scene list is a chronological list of scenes, not your outline, not the work you did before writing, but **a simple list of the scenes you've actually written.** This will help separate what you planned to write, what you think you wrote, and what you actually wrote, and give you a chance to get a fresh angle on the basics of your screenplay.

For example: Here's a partial scene list from an early draft of a new script of mine called *Reborn.*

Introduce Rome - Night

Introduce four young men drinking

Surprise, the young men are priests

Drunken young men in Rome fountain

Terence in papal gardens

Terence has vision

In the morning, gardener discovers
sleepy Terence

Terence rushing to Vatican job

Late for job, tries to tell pal of
vision

Each of the scenes—representing seven total pages of screen-play—is a conceptual reminder of what I've written. I just *scan* the pages, getting the idea of the scene so I can put it on the scene list. I'll *read* the screenplay later. The scene descriptions are purposely brief so I don't get involved in the details of the writing or story-telling. **I want to think about the script in conceptual blocks.** In that way, I can relook at the screenplay as a whole, the big strokes.

This process of listing scenes gets me thinking about the basics of the story. I do see things differently after I've stepped away.

At this point, I may move scenes around or delete scenes that suddenly, with this new perspective, seem irrelevant. I do the work in the scene list first. Then, after I've made all the changes that I want, I make those changes in the screenplay.

Another way to get a new slant on your screenplay is to color and shape code different elements in your scene list. Red for action. Blue for dialogue. Diamonds for the hero. Boxes for the antagonist. A heart for the girlfriend. A circle for scenes with humor, and so on.

I put a code or codes to the left of each scene; then, when I'm finished, I tape the scene list pages together, top to bottom, push-pin it up on the wall, then "read the codes." This allows me to "see" the movie by the different rhythms of the shapes and colors, the basics of the screenplay. You'll see if your hero is not in enough scenes, if the girlfriend has disappeared for too long, if there are too many action scenes too close together. *Coding is an incredible tool for getting perspective.* If it isn't a coded scene list, its three-by-five cards; whatever the tools, getting perspective is the goal.

When I've finished charting the movie and absorbing it, I'm ready to read the damn thing word for word.

I try to approach this first read as much like a fresh reader as I possibly can. I don't read it on the computer. I don't read it with a pen in my hand (that quickly changes, but I try). I choose a location different than the place I wrote the screenplay. I try and read the screenplay as if I've just picked it up at the local screenplay store— if only—and I'm going to read it to pass a few hours.

I try and read the script at one sitting, no writing, no distractions. If a rewrite does come to mind, and it inevitably does, I just make a note of it and don't do it.

When I finish reading, I gather my thoughts and write any further rewrite ideas down. After that, rewrite notes in hand, I'm ready to begin the actual rewriting.

My Usual Reaction When I Read My Rough Draft?

I'm pleased and disappointed. Pleased because I usually don't remember much of what I've written so I'm occasionally really surprised at the writing or a twist of the story, and that's great. I'm disappointed because I always want the writing to be better. I want it to be as good as the original thought, the initial flush of excitement that prompted "That's a good idea for a movie" in my head. If I can reach that moment and extend it for the length of the screenplay, I'm there. It's daunting.

It's what drives me as a rewriter.

Secret #2:
Prioritizing the Big Scenes

Call them big, or important, or key, whatever you want, but **make a list of the big scenes, the most important first.** It could be four, it could be ten. Usually they're the key dialogue scenes that turn the story or explain the characters. They may be the major set-piece action scenes, the big love scenes, the murder scenes. They are the scenes people will remember in your screenplay/movie. They are the scenes that will grab a reader and get your script produced.

Frank Capra said you need four such big scenes, but that was many years ago and times change. The pace that films are cut these days—influenced by TV, video games, music videos, the evolution of the art and technology of editing—has sped up the editorial pace of storytelling.

The result? An audience's appetite and expectation for more: more action, more big scenes, *more*, faster—the roller coaster. Today's theatrical feature market is driven by the twelve-through-twenty-four age bracket and the results are tent-pole action/comic-book franchises. The roller coaster experience needs for that genre are high. Those audiences have an appetite for big action movies and that's what the studios are delivering.

Needless to say, the more important scenes you have in this roller coaster storytelling world the better. When I saw *The Day After To-morrow*, Roland Emmerich's global warming blockbuster, I was as much astounded by the magnificent state-of-the-art effects as I was about the paucity of human stories. It felt to me there were ten drafts of writing on the special effects and the human stories were still in rough draft. Call in the rewriters.

A way to think about the prioritizing of the scenes is to **think how a studio would market your film,** what the trailer and TV spots would be. Those scenes are what make up your list.

I believe one of the key reasons for the success of a film I wrote called *Stigmata* was MGM's extraordinary television campaign. There were enough intriguing scenes to make a terrific trailer.

Finally, once you have your list of prioritized scenes, study it. See how the scenes relate to each other. What you're looking for is an **arc.** The scenes should start good and evolve to great. They should start small and get bigger and better. There should be a build so that the reader/viewer is fed more and more as they go along. This keeps the reader/viewer tuned in. It's called **rising action.** If your arc is flat and the reader/viewer is getting more of the same, scene after scene, they tune out.

Rising action is a concept that works across genres. In a love story, the relationship must progress or stagnate. In a murder mystery, the number of corpses has to build. In action movies, the stunts have to get bigger and better.

This evolving arc is vital to keeping the reader/viewer hooked into your script.

Secret #3:
Tracking the Transitions

This third focused rewrite specifically targets how scenes end and how they begin and how the transition between them works.

Read only the beginnings and ends of scenes and visualize how they will look as they transition from one to the next.

I believe the mind "sees" the movie as you read it and *a bad visual cut on the written page will read badly in the mind of the reader.*

Do I have proof of this?

Am I a brain researcher?

Well, I've written brain researchers for TV.

Transitions are one of the keys to writing smooth-reading screenplays. Rewriting transitions goes a long way to evolving your screenplay.

Feedback on my writing is pretty much always the same: "It was a smooth read." "It was a page-turner, I couldn't put it down." Good transitions are a major factor in getting back comments like these.

For example, a not so good transition:

INT. ST. PETER'S BASILICA - DAY

Father Terence jumps over the small railing and,
unbelievably, climbs up on the crucifix and kisses the
wound of Christ. It immediately starts bleeding . . .
real blood . . . dripping on Father Terence.
Security personnel grab the bloody father, pull him
off the statue, and hustle him out past the wide-eyed
tourists. He's disoriented and confused.

INT. VATICAN PALAZZO DE GIUSTIZIA - DAY

Father Terence sits in front of the elderly
CONSIGLIORE, who studies Father Terence as he talks.

   Now, a more cinematic, brain-pleasing version:

INT. ST. PETER'S BASILICA - DAY

Father Terence jumps over the small railing and,
unbelievably, climbs up on the crucifix and kisses the
wound of Christ . . .
. . . And it starts bleeding . . .
. . . dripping . . . onto Father Terence.
Security personnel grab the bloody father, who is
disoriented and confused, and pull him off the
statue . . . they hustle him out past the wide-eyed
tourists.

EXT. VATICAN PALAZZO DE GIUSTIZIA - DAY

The age-stained marble facade wet from the rain.

INT. VATICAN CONSIGLIORE PSICOLOGIA - DAY

A mahogany-lined office. Leather-bound books in
bookcases. Modern religious art. A tense Father

```
Terence sits in front of the elderly CONSIGLIORE, who
studies Father Terence as he talks.
```

The first version is workmanlike, rough draft stuff, with a "Father Terence" to "Father Terence" cut, which is not very visual.

The second version sells mood and place, cuts from Father Terence to the new place he is, to the specific office he's in; it's a moment for the reader/viewer to catch their breath—and then to resume Father Terence's story. It's the rewrite.

One of the best transitions is when you're cutting from a wide shot to a tight shot, or vice versa.

It's the difference between the shots that makes the good cut. The better the transition, the better the read, the better the movie.

Simply put, badly executed transitions lessen your chances that the reader will buy your screenplay. Motivation enough?

And if you don't pay close attention to transitions? You'll burn in hell and your screenplay will be used to wrap fish. No, but I believe your screenplay will be more difficult to read, if not on a conscious level, a subconscious level.

Everything counts.

Secret #4:
Plotting Corrections

List all of your proposed rewrites for your script. Categorize them according to the type and kind of rewrite it is.

In my writing the most common rewrites are:

1. *Move the character name from the first word of the sentence to after a parenthetical phrase.* For example: "Father Terence, running from the police, ducks into the shadows." Rewritten to: "Running from the police, Father Terence ducks into the shadows." The rewrite has a simple, more elegant rhythm.

2. *Up the emotions in the most emotional scenes.* I seem to be severely limited emotionally—ask my ex-wives—and that comes back to haunt me in my writing. I'm always having to crank up the emotion in my rewrites. The first time this was brought to my attention was when I was writing a movie of the week for CBS about a gay couple moving into a quiet suburban neighborhood. (This was a number of years ago. Now I guess it would be about a gay marriage in a quiet suburban neighborhood.) I wrote a scene where one of my heroes, in response to stress, fell asleep. The producer—who was very kind to me about this—told me I should try some behavior that would be a little more cinematic, like blowing up, or freaking out, or breaking something, or swearing. Something, *anything,* but having the guy fall asleep. The producer was, of course, totally correct. Not so coincidentally, when I'm stressed out I tend to fall asleep.

3. *Take out the first line in dialogue because it usually mirrors the last line.* I find on my rough drafts, many times I'll begin the dialogue with what I think I want the character to say. Then, in the course of writing it, I discover exactly what I want the characters say. I usually eliminate where I started and cut out the opening line.

4. *Remove the last line of stage direction in the scene because it's usually anticlimatic.* I've already written the drama and the last line of stage direction may work on screen to get the character or story accelerating into the next scene by putting a visual cap to the scene, but on the page, it usually feels tacked on and anticlimactic.

5. *Make the scenes deeper, rounder, and more mature in little, step-by-step increments.* My rewriting approach is additive. I do lots of drafts, adding little bits, corrections, making it richer and more detailed, one rewrite leading to another. It's like pulling teeth, but that's the only way I really get it done.

Other writers I know mature a scene before they move on to the next scene. I prefer the incremental approach because it keeps me writing with the flow of the screenplay. I don't think one is better than the other. It's a matter of which works better for you.

When you've plotted the kinds of corrections you usually make, you'll more than likely begin to see a pattern. Then, design a rewrite that addresses those issues only.

Becoming aware of your most common mistakes and addressing them off the top is a way to shortcut your normal rewriting process.

No matter how much I'm aware of my most common mistakes, in the heat of writing, when I'm really flying, I still make the same mistakes. Even after all these years. Mini-rewrite #4 is designed to combat that.

Secret #5:
New Information

This mini-rewrite of your script is vital.

Analyze each scene independently and figure out what new information is carried in the scene. Write it down. Make a list. This way, you're forced to examine if, in fact, a scene moves the story forward. If it doesn't, then you seriously have to evaluate if the scene is worth keeping.

What are scenes that move the story forward?

Simply put, any scene that gives the reader/viewer new information, a new story beat, an evolution of a relationship, a playing out of a story thread.

My experience in the editing room is that scenes that don't move the story forward, that are treading water story-wise, that have nothing new in them, end up on the cutting room floor. Every time.

I believe there should be very few, if any, rules of screenwriting.

I preach that you should try and write outside of the box. Try new things. Experiment. Take chances. Develop an original voice rather than ape the writer-of-the-week's style. But—and this is a big "but"—one of those rules of both writing and rewriting is: **If a scene doesn't move the story forward cut it or rewrite it so it does move the story forward.**

Though not strictly about rewriting, the following is the single most important idea you can learn in this book.

One of the keys to making a script a page-turner in any genre is the careful and premeditated disclosure of information while always promising more information. It is the balance of the two elements—the continuing dissemination of information and the continuing tease of even more intriguing stuff to come—that makes the reader curious and want to, *have to,* turn the page.

New writers have a tendency to hold back vital story information to create mystery and intrigue, and then blurt out all the juicy stuff at the end of the screenplay. This might work in a novel, but only causes confusion in a screenplay and is ultimately an unsatisfying way to tell a story. It is the steady stream of new information that holds the reader/viewer's attention.

Think about your scenes in the context of how much information have you disclosed and how much more is there to go. Graph them. Write them down. Analyze them. Think about them. It's what makes screenplays good.

Come up with a list plotting the page numbers when and where your key information is presented.

Check the frequency of disclosure to make sure it is correctly spaced, that you're giving the reader a constant stream of new material while still promising them more to come.

It is vital to a readable, involving, and satisfying screenplay.

Secret #6:
The Dialogue Pass

Read your dialogue out loud.

I'll say it again.

Read your dialogue out loud.

If you can, have someone read it to you, so you can actually hear what it sounds like. Go to a local theater group; ask if they'll do a workshop reading of your screenplay.

Ask your writer's group—or any writer's group—to do a reading for you. Your actors/readers will let you know if they have trouble understanding the meaning of what they're saying or reading.

Your ear will tell you which dialogue needs rewriting.

It's that simple.

It's that important.

When I'm holding casting auditions for 7 *Lives Xposed,* the cable series I write, direct, and executive produce, I rotate sides—the script pages the actors are reading—so I can hear the actors read different parts of the script, so I can *hear* it. I also hold table readings on the Thursday before the Monday we begin shooting new episodes. I invariably hear a dialogue clinker, or repetitive words, or unspeakable sentences, or jokes that don't work, and have time to do a quick final production polish before we shoot.

Listen to people talk—at the next table in restaurants, on buses, waiting on line for the movies. Listen to the run of words. The pauses. The specific words they use. The combination of words. The rhythms. The things they don't say. Where they laugh in the sentence.

Good dialogue is about good listening.

Secret #7:
On-the-Nose Rewrite

This one's a little tougher.

For this draft, sit down and read the script.

Yes, again.

I can hear some of you out there bellyaching about having to read the script so many times. "What is this guy, crazy? How many times can a person read a script?" *Especially* when that person wrote it in the first place?

The deal is: Every time I read my script, I rewrite it and make it better. **That's every time I read my script, I rewrite it and make it better.**

Now, back to the On-the-Nose Draft. Don't read for flow, or grammar, or action, but for *how much your characters are saying exactly what they mean.* This is a hard concept.

In my advanced screenwriting class at UCLA Extension in Los Angeles, where I've been teaching for the last thirteen years, one of my students, writing an interesting screenplay, wrote a scene I thought was on the nose.

```
INT. CLASSROOM - DAY

Professor Richardson closes his book.

            PROFESSOR RICHARDSON
        OK, everyone, I'm going to give out
        papers.

Melinda doesn't look up from her doodling. Professor
Richardson hands out papers in the first row, then
gives Melinda her paper.

            PROFESSOR RICHARDSON
               (continued)
        Melinda . . . great work.

Her paper has a big red A+ on it.
```

My note to the writer was that the scene was on the nose. The professor might as well have walked up to Melinda and said, "You're very smart," or, better yet, looked into camera and said, "Melinda's very smart." That was the information the writer wanted the scene to carry and, by God, those characters said it exactly like that. Melinda was smart. Well, it was made very clear. Too clear. It was on the nose.

The challenge for the writer is, how best can you divert the reader so the message "Melinda is smart" isn't so obvious, that it's understood, but it's presented a little more subtly?

Use subtext. It is a more interesting way to write. It has more resonance. It asks more of the reader/viewer. It gives them more to do because it's reading between the lines, figuring out what the characters are really thinking or feeling. It involves them more. Subtext will elevate your screenplay and ultimately your movie.

Here's a less on-the-nose rewrite of the same scene:

```
INT. UNIVERSITY HALLWAY - DAY

Melinda walks by the students crowding around the
lists of marks stapled on the bulletin board. Tawny
sees her.

                    TAWNY
          You got an A.

                    MELINDA
          I give a shit.

                    TAWNY
          You were the only A in class.

                    MELINDA
          Bitch!

And she heads out. Tawny shakes her head.
```

Now there's more—Melinda's attitude, the aggression, the miss—something else going on in the scene other than just the information you want the scene to carry. Something that makes the reader/viewer intrigued, curious about the characters.

Try this.

Take your favorite unsold script and ask yourself these questions:

Could this script be better after a rewrite?

What are the main things to be rewritten? (You can list these by subject, or scenes, or dialogue, or characters.)

Do I care enough about this script to rewrite it?

Wouldn't it be great if you could take one of your scripts and make it measurably better by employing this Strategy for Rewriting?

Rewriting is how you make your writing better.

The more you rewrite your script, the better it gets.

Getting perspective, a new point of view, a fresh look is valuable.

Employ this Strategy for Rewriting enough so that it becomes an integral part of your screenwriting process, that it becomes a single, multifaceted rewrite where you combine the seven mini-rewrites into one.

Your scripts will be better for it every time.

NOTE: For now, resist the temptation to combine some of the steps to save time.

It's the process that's important here.

From good process comes a good screenplay.

Three

THE WRITER IS IN THE ROOM

RECEIVING REWRITE NOTES IS ONE OF THE MOST DIFFICULT things a screenwriter can experience. The pain is second only to childbirth. Well . . . maybe kidney stones.

Sensitive, aware producers usually open a notes meeting with a compliment: "Really well written." "We're really on our way now." "This is terrific work . . . we couldn't be happier." I don't care if they're lying. I don't care if they don't mean it. At least, on some level, by opening with a positive comment, they're being considerate about my feelings, and that counts. It's fine. That's smart. They've calmed me down because, at the beginning of these meetings, I am tense. Most writers are. I've put a lot of time into the script they're reading and I'm anxious/concerned/nervous about their response. After they've made me feel good, I'm much more receptive to their notes and we get down to specifics. Because they've cared about my feelings, my goal is to make *them* feel good by being open and responsive. That meeting will be collegial, friendly, productive, and good things will come of it.

On the flip side, however, there are the other producers or agents who don't care about the writer's feelings, who take this opportunity to diminish the writer, to use their position to run roughshod over writers to make themselves feel competent and on top. It's a hard part of the game.

I think rewrite notes and contract negotiating—other than the constant threat of failure and starvation—are the two most difficult tasks for screenwriters.

A note about negotiations: They can be brutal. They can make you feel bad, as the person negotiating for the producers will say anything—the more hurtful the better—to get your price down. One of the most important functions of an agent is to shelter their clients from such abuse.

The issue is separating yourself from the work. My strong suit is my passion, how I invest myself in the screenplay lock, stock, and barrel. The downside is that I get too invested, take things too personally, and do stupid things in rewrite meetings. I have sulked. I've gotten nasty. I've become defensive. I've made it uncomfortable for the other people in the room. I've been a jerk. My worst offense to date? In a rough-cut notes meeting with my clients and their marketing people, I kicked the back of the chair of the marketing executive because he was critical of the film. Within three weeks, I was fired. Not so good.

Headline: "SCREENWRITER SHOOTS SELF IN FOOT, BECOMES OSTRACIZED!"

Some producers do their homework, work with their development people or make notes by themselves and present typed-up, logical changes. They say not only *what* but *why*. I like those producers. They respect the work and me, and do their job. They play fair and that's great. If there were only more of them.

Too many notes sessions in my experience, however, are much different. Most producers will have read the draft. Some will try and fake it and not cop to the fact that someone has read the script for them. They will only partially be able to articulate what they feel the problems are.

One producer, actually a really nice guy, led off our notes meeting by asking me if I thought this was my best work.

If I had said yes, then, when he hated the script—which he did—I wouldn't be able to do better; or if I said no, then why did I hand in less than my best work.

I didn't answer.

How did it make me feel? Unsure, nervous, insecure, defensive.

Was that his intent? Was this his opening, softening-up gambit? Hard to say, but I have my suspicions.

In the meeting, I was resistant to his notes. Human nature, I guess. The picture never got made.

In addition to pointing out the problems, a lot of producers try to solve them. This happens a great deal of the time and in my mind is problematic and dangerous. Tell me the problems and I'll solve them. I'm the writer. I'm happy to listen and use what's good, but don't present "the answers" to me as gospel. I think producers feel impotent if they just point out the problems. Sometimes they suggest good things. Many times they don't.

THE CURSE OF SPITBALLING

I deal with spitballing in most notes meetings. Spitballing is when the producer, in a convulsion of creativity, puts his pristine, nonroll, air-cushioned, never-been-run-in running shoes up on the Joel Silver model, faux Craftsman desk and weaves an incoherent, often inarticulate and illogical tale that, with the support of his nodding development toadies, he or she believes, somehow, will solve all of the draft's problems. I listen. I make notes. I nod my head. I agree whenever I can. My favorite response in a notes meeting is "I'll take a look at it." Can they ask more? I think not.

> NOTE: Please excuse the vitriol of the previous paragraph. I'm working out some issues.

I try never to commit to a rewrite on anything in a notes meeting.

If I've agreed on a note in a meeting and it's not working during the rewrite, what do I do? I will call the producer or development person and tell them what's happening. They're the client. The idea is to satisfy them without sacrificing the integrity of the project.

Four

SCRIPT NOTES FROM HELL

I'VE GOTTEN SCRIPT NOTES ON THE PHONE FROM A DIS-
tracted producer incessantly and rudely taking other calls.

I've gotten script notes from producers babysitting their two
screaming and puking kids.

I've gotten script notes while a producer ordered a CD changer
for his BMW.

I've gotten script notes on a producer's boat while topless girls
drank chi-chis in the sun all around us.

I've gotten script notes around pools, in almost every model
Mercedes Benz, and in every single deli in the greater Los Angeles
metropolitan area.

Getting Notes Is an Exercise in Patience

As I've said, being on the receiving end of rewrite notes is hard. It's
so important and very few people, writers or note givers, do it well.
Writers get defensive. Producers get offensive. Sides are drawn,
communication and the work suffer, and the meetings are generally
not as productive as they should be. Let me give you a couple of examples.

EXAMPLE ONE

I'm working on the third year of my series. Each previous season, the characters that live together in a house bring their private cars. One of my production executives—my boss—spitballed an idea: "Instead of them driving their own cars, let's have them arrive in a limousine!" The notes meeting we were having was particularly heated—more about being right than making the script better— and this seemed like an innocuous enough idea, so I said sure. Let's make it easy.

Well, talk about something coming back and biting me in the butt. It turned out that when we shot the show the roommates didn't have their own cars, so when they had to go anywhere, we had to hire a cab, a cabdriver, a couple limousines, and drivers. Cost our production budget a whole lot more, instead of using the actor's or crew's cars as we had in the past.

The Ripple Factor

One of things to remember about rewriting is, if you make a change, you must be sure to track it forward and back through the script, so everything remains consistent.

EXAMPLE TWO

I was writing a science-fiction movie for a cable network. I was told by the production executive at a major studio—a very bright, very nice woman—that I was the "talent" of this deal and that I should "bring the neophyte producers along with me." I was the Eight-Hundred-Pound Gorilla and I felt good about it. Lots of hard work had gotten me to this place in my career and I was enjoying it and feeling confident about my writing.

The two producers—one, let's call him Jerry, was best known as a regular on a TV series; the other was an Ugly Little Man, a director of family television sitcoms, whose name has been expunged from my brain—were new to development and it showed. We were up-dating a sci-fi classic owned by the studio and were trying to bring new, contemporary, and affordable-for-cable elements to it. I was hired by the studio. They were thrilled to work with me and I with them.

I came into the first meeting with the studio, the producers, and executive producers with my pages: the log line, characters, the seven act breaks, the main character's arc, the big production scenes. I had my pitch memorized. I'd pitched it to my (then) wife and (then) dogs for two days. I had hard copies—a leave-behind—of my ideas for everyone. The pages weren't labeled outline or beat sheet but pitch notes, so everyone's expectations about them remained low.

> NOTE: *Leave-behinds* are a good idea because many times you won't be meeting with the person who is ultimately making the decision. If you don't leave behind, that means the person you met with has to repitch your idea to their boss based on their memory and notes, if any. So much opportunity for human error. I prefer to control the material, so I give them pages for the executive to read, or, at least, have pitch notes so the development person pitches from them.

I hadn't met the two executive producers—the financial guarantors—before. They were powerful, nice, and respectful. I guess they could be, they controlled the money. Also at the meeting: Jerry and the Ugly Little Man. I pitched and everyone bought it. They were thrilled. There were some suggestions. Nothing major. Everyone loved me. I loved everyone. Perfect. I was on my way.

Headline: "WORTHY WRITER IS LOVED—WINS EMMY!"

Back in the parking lot and still flushed with success, I arranged with Jerry and the Ugly Little Man to have a story meeting just to make sure we were all on the same page.

We met at Jerry's house in Los Angeles. Rural, big, really nice. He'd done a lot of the masonry work himself and he was good. Jerry turned out to be a nice, reasonable, conciliatory man, and the

Ugly Little Man turned out to be the jerk of all time. The ULM immediately announced they were unhappy with what everyone, including them, had agreed to. They wanted to "explore new ideas." Confident that I was going to do whatever I wanted, being the Eight-Hundred-Pound Gorilla and all, I magnanimously said "Sure."

What proceeded was a cascading nightmare of the Ugly Little Man's what-if scenarios:

"What if the hero was a woman?"

"What if the hero was a psychiatrist?"

"What if he was in a wheelchair?"

"What if he was really an alien?"

"What if he's an alien and doesn't know he's an alien?"

"What if he's an alien, but turns out to be human?"

"What if the dog's an alien?"

Hour after hour. Meeting after meeting. Spitballed idea after spitballed idea. We never got anywhere. The lack of progress was melting my brain.

"What if *everyone* turns out to be an alien?"

"What if the children were conduits for the aliens?"

"What if everyone's skin falls off?"

What if the producers drive the writer bonkers? They were. I was working for major studio money and I was the Eight-Hundred-Pound Gorilla. But it was hurting me. I figured I'd humor them just a little longer, then go away and write.

For the fifth meeting, with the studio's words "You're the talent, do what you want" growing fainter and fainter in my head, I had created a new outline based on my original pages with a few of the ideas that I squeezed in from our recent marathon of meetings. Jerry thought it was "fine," but the ULM had some more thoughts. Some more questions. Some more what-ifs.

I balked.

The ULM asked, "Aren't you open to new ideas?"

I said of course I was and we continued.

The more they free-associated new, spitballed ideas, the more upset I became. Finally, with my body literally shaking—I was as close to having what they used to call in movies a nervous breakdown as

I'd ever been in my life—I left the room and went outside, calmed myself by breathing. Long and deep. Long and deep.

Overwhelmed and short-circuiting, I was so close to walking out on the project. I felt assaulted and under attack. They ganged up on me and it worked. They broke me. I listened to the ULM prattle on for a while more, then said I'd come in with a draft, and fled.

I wrote the script. As usual I got into it. Loved the process as always. The pain of the nightmare spitball meetings gave way to the joys of writing, of creative problem solving, of creative discovery.

After a ton of rewriting, I proudly delivered the first draft to Jerry and the Ugly Little Man before we sent it on to the studio.

When I got Jerry and ULM's notes, they were totally off the wall. Whole new ideas, new characters, contradictory notes: in effect, starting over again.

I couldn't believe it. I think they were way over their heads and rather than commit to something and move forward, they were creatively frozen. Unsure of themselves, they couldn't make a decision for fear of failing and returning to family TV rerun oblivion. After not agreeing to anything, I went screaming off into the California night.

I did another draft incorporating a few of their rewrite notes, but didn't do the page-one rewrite they were looking for. Continuing to view them as my partners, I turned the rewrite in to the producers for their final-polish notes before we gave it to the studio so we could go to the studio as a united front.

They had no notes.

None.

Not one note.

I was dumbfounded. After all of their hocking me with new ideas and things that didn't work, they now had no notes? None? We submitted it to the studio. I should have been smarter.

I found out later from my agent, the producers went to the studio and said it was them or me. They hated the draft and couldn't work with me.

My pals at the studio, the people who had told me to do what I want, that I was the talent, when push came to shove sided with Jerry and the Ugly Little Man—who they had an overall deal with—and I was off the project.

Jerry and the Ugly Little Man, neither of them writers, went on to write the next draft themselves.

I love Hollywood.

Needless to say, the film never got made.

Headline: "STUDIO SHOOTS SELF IN FOOT. SCRIPT LOST!"

PLAN B—POSITIVE REINFORCEMENT

On the first day of one recent series job, I had a meeting with the executive responsible for the show. We'd worked together before and it had been relatively contentious, but we had pretty much moved beyond that. I said "The way to get the best writing from me is to make me feel good. Positive reinforcement makes me feel good, and when I feel good I'll write to the last breath for you."

He was supportive. He was encouraging. He would go out of his way to make the nice comment. We went on to create over sixty hours of successful programming together.

Positive reinforcement—making someone feel good about the job their doing—works.

It increases productivity.

It increases the quality of the work.

Why don't more people do it?

A MOMENT OF CLARITY

As you've probably gathered, most of the time in notes meetings I have to fight the urge to leap across the table and tear the note giver's face off. I'm not proud of this. It's uncomfortable at times. I do my best, which, unfortunately, is not very good at all. I struggle to be better at it, but usually lose.

The people giving you notes are your partners. Listen to them.

They have a right to their opinions and if you, as I have, make them feel uncomfortable when they give you notes, they won't want to work with you again. There are a lot of smiling, pleasant, talented writers out there all too willing to do whatever producers want.

Headline: "SCREENWRITER HEARS FOOTSTEPS, RUNS FASTER"

Five

GOOD REWRITE NOTES

THERE IS A LONG TRADITION OF SCREENWRITERS ASKING FOR notes from fellow screenwriters. I do it. Lots of writers do it. **What is the right way to give rewrite notes? It's simple: be caring, be sensitive, and be prepared.**

One of the biggest mistakes note givers make is giving notes *outside the story*. For example, the writer has written a thriller. The note giver's idea is that it should be a musical. Not helpful.

Give Notes That Are Inside the Story

Respond to what is on the page, not what you think should be there or how you would tell the story if you had the chance. Tell the truth, but limit it to constructive, inside-the-story comments. The scriptwriter has already made the basic foundation decisions. Respect them.

There are occasional exceptions. I recently asked for notes from a writer friend, first time I had asked him. It was a science fiction script. He said it was funny and should be a comedy. I tried it and it worked.

HINT: Ask the writer what kind of notes they're looking for, what script the writer was trying to write, so you know how to focus your notes.

When I'm hired to consult on a script, I present my rewrite notes to the writer in three parts.

1. Big notes:
   Is the script worth rewriting? Is it well written enough to be considered? Is the idea good enough? Is there a market for this script?
   Is the script salable? Makable? Castable?
   Consider the writing issues: Style, Format, Film Language. Is the script consistent? Is it appropriate?
   What's the big flaw? Will it even be possible to fix it?
   Are there structural problems? Usually, the first act is too long, the second act sags, and the third disappoints.
   Does the script start in the right place? Most early drafts need the first ten to thirty pages lopped off.

2. Specific notes:
   Character arcs that aren't arcing
   Transitions that don't work
   Voices sounding too similar

Because of my experience, people hire me to critique scripts; I make suggestions for how to fix things.

3. The fix:
   Conceptual issues
   What's the movie?
   What should it be?
   Specific issues of style:
      1. punctuation
      2. dialogue
      3. minor writing issues

The Most Common Rewrite Note, Particularly with New Writers?

A lot of scripts open with too much backstory, too much setup, and introductory exposition. My advice is start the story, hook the reader, *then* do your backstory.

GOOD REWRITE NOTES

The thirteen hours of dramatic programming a year I create for my cable series 7 *Lives Xposed* is one of the great gigs of all time. I get to write the equivalent of six movies a year. I've just finished shooting my fifth year. The downside is I don't have many sounding boards. I'm doing so much of the creative work myself, the danger is I become lost, have tunnel vision, lose perspective, get too big a head, and think I'm infallible. That's when good, constructive rewrite notes are necessary.

For each season, I write an average of five drafts on thirteen hours, over seven hundred pages of finished, shootable teleplay. The two executives in charge of the series, Sol Weisel and Eric Deutsch, give me notes every step along the way, as does my long-suffering wife, Stevie, who is the only other writer on the show.

Sol and Eric and I are not totally on the same page, but we've done the dance so many times and there's enough mutual respect, that the process, though not always easy, is an incredibly productive one. We really are partners. The rewriting experience can be a good one.

ANOTHER RARE MOMENT OF CLARITY

In the fourth year of collaborating with these two executives, I had a moment of clarity about them. Their notes, in large part, can be categorized as "make it more on the nose." They were always telling me to "explain it more." "Hit it on the head." "Set it up." "Give it some context." "Have someone say something about it." It always makes me a little crazy. Then I had the insight: *They don't trust images alone to carry information, feelings, or story.*

That, suddenly, explained everything. They needed every character to *say* what they were doing, rather than letting the audience *see* the behavior and understand the story by experiencing it, rather than being told about it. Well-meaning and bright, the executives don't trust that **images—without words—can sometimes more powerfully convey story and character than hearing**

someone say something about it. They are in the TV business but have no faith in the basic nature of the medium.

This moment of clarity hasn't really changed how we do our dance. I write them more on-the-nose stuff—some of it works, some of it ends up on the cutting-room floor.

Six

REWRITING THE BEGINNING OF AN IDEA

HOUSE OF PAIN—A CASE STUDY

THE IDEA FOR THE MOVIE JUST POPPED UP IN MY HEAD.

Inspired by the success of the Joan Crawford and Bette Davis movie *Whatever Happened to Baby Jane?* I'd write a Gothic terror script for Meryl Streep and Glenn Close. Two great actors strutting their stuff. I loved it. *WHTBJ?*, directed by Robert Aldrich, was fun and made money, and had great performances by two superb icons. Not so bad. We haven't seen anything like that in a while.

When using another movie or book or play as inspiration for a project you're writing, make sure your idea is far enough away from the original that no one will say, "That's another so-and-so." *Stigmata* was inspired by the box-office success of *The Exorcist*, but it was a totally different movie.

The first time I tried writing *House of Pain* it was the story of a film director who died leaving his mansion in Hollywood to his two ex-wives and his present wife. Three strong women, all of whom occupy the house thinking it's theirs.

I got about thirty pages into *House of Pain* and hated it. It was phony, no real behavior, no real anything. It turned out the conceit didn't work. I didn't believe for one second that those women would be doing what they were doing so I abandoned the script. Not easy, but necessary.

Then I opened my mind to a new version of the idea. I knew it had to be smart if I had a chance of attracting actresses of the quality of Streep and Close. Hey, if it wasn't hard, it wouldn't be any fun. Though it was a little daunting that a smart, layered, thoughtful script was needed to get them. It's the challenge.

So I thought about the idea. Then I sat down and wrote the first spine version of the movie, from beginning to end, fast all at once. Here it is. . . .

House of Pain
by Tom Lazarus

Introduce artist Glenn in her life. Vibrant. Alive. Independent.

Meryl has been taking care of Mama since her fall in 1988.

There was talk of Mama faking her injuries, Glenn said she was, but Meryl believed her and took care of her, in the family house, until now, when she appears to be dying.

At the doctor's suggestion, Meryl calls Glenn; it's time to come home.

Glenn comes home . . . and it's the nightmare.

She stays in her old room.

And falls into old ways.

It becomes intolerable. . . .

Then Mama dies.

The funeral.

Going through things, Glenn begins finding things.

Piles of unopened, unread letters addressed to Mama from her, other people.

Meryl denies everything.

Bloody rags.

Stories of Mama's craziness.

Mama's journal. Which Glenn reads to Meryl.

Then Meryl attacks Glenn, knocks her out.

Glenn wakes up . . . she's strapped to the bed.

And Meryl is who she wants to be . . .

Who she was with Mama.

The Caretaker. In charge.

And Meryl takes care of Glenn . . .

Feeds her . . .

Gets angry at her . . .

Tortures her.

And Glenn realizes Meryl killed their mother . . .

And is going to kill her.

Because Meryl is psychotic.

A killer.

She killed their father . . .

Their mother . . .

And now her.

But Glenn fights back . . .

And is about to escape, but doesn't.

And things get worse.

Much worse.

Until Glenn figures it out . . .

Tricks Meryl.

And Glenn is victorious

And Meryl is the Big loser.

The End

This was the first time through. The rush of the idea. The creative burst.

The idea needs to be layered, to be smartened up, other incidents and characters have to be brought in, the story has to wrinkle up (more twists and turns), elements of surprise put in, scariness, weirdness put in, but as the initial rush of the idea, it's really exciting.

I've taken this journey before. I've written over fifty completed screenplays—and maybe a dozen more written in whole or in part, then abandoned. Now I was at the beginning of the idea. Always the part that's the most fun. The creative leaps are the most exciting. Seeing whole passages of the film. Seeing it as a conceptual whole, rather than bogged down by the creative minutiae.

What Did I Have to Look Forward To?

Fun.

Creative problem solving.

The journey of discovering and maximizing this idea.

Of trying my hardest to reach the potential of this idea.

Of writing and rewriting something good and smart and exciting and scary and surprising and successful and living happily ever after.

It's how it starts.

Headline: "SCREENWRITER LOVES LIFE!"

NOTE: I haven't applied the tried-and-true three-act structure to this idea. I haven't plotted out the turning points, or inciting incidents. I haven't figured out character arcs or created character biographies. I have told the story shooting from the hip, because I believe in the integrity of the story, that it will tell itself in the way it should. At some point, I'm sure I'll apply the three-act structure to the idea, at least to analyze it.

To some degree, just my knowledge of the three-act structure informs my thinking, informs my storytelling. It's the same way I'm hoping this book, these stories, and these examples inform your rewriting process.

Before doing any more rewrites, trying to "stay away" from the idea for a while, I create character biographies. For a script that calls out for rich, complex, multilayered characters, I think character biographies are an absolute necessity.

This is always fun. I never censor anything. I draw from my life, my experiences, anything I've read or heard about, anything that's stuck in the festering crevices of my memory. I change it. I spin it. I add or subtract to it, so I can ultimately make it my own.

Of course, I have the models of Glenn Close and Meryl Streep. What I know of them, on screen and off, but I don't want to write it too specifically for them. That's too nuts.

I Have to Mention My Sanity at This Point

Do I believe, actually believe, Meryl Streep and Glenn Close are on the phone with each other, bemoaning the fact they don't have the latest draft of my script? I don't think so. But I do believe it's a good thing to have a strategy, to have a bigger view of my script than just the writing of it.

It's the Process

My deal as a writer, and sometime writer/director, is it's the process. It's the doing of what I do that's important to me. The product less so.

What that means is number one: I'll write it, that's creative problem solving. Then, number two is to get it made. And how, or at what level: studio movie, independent feature, TV Movie of the Week, cable movie, it doesn't really make a difference to me. I keep turning the scripts out. And if they get made, fine, but *it's the process of writing—the part I can actually control—that is what I invest myself in.*

The rest?

Out of my hands.

HOUSE OF PAIN
CHARACTER BIOGRAPHIES
(ROUGH DRAFT)

PAMELA, Meryl at the moment, has been taking care of her mother since 1988. She was born in 1954 and is dangerously close to the big five-oh.

Graduated high school in 1971. She was a good student. Not very social. Hung out with girlfriends. Always looked at guys, all unrealized sexuality.

Went to a really good school, Sarah Lawrence, studied art history, graduated in 1975.

Then she worked at Bennington Potters, and a month after meeting a lawyer named Barry, Pamela married him.

She was unable to have children . . . no matter how she tried . . . and after five years of marriage in 1980, Barry had an affair with another lawyer in his office and got caught, exposed, and he ran off with the other woman. He died six months later.

Pamela's been fighting depression ever since.

In 1982 there was a suicide attempt.

And things continued going bad.

She went on medication in 1984 . . . then stopped taking it.

Her father was killed in 1985.

In 1986, after losing her job due to erratic behavior, Pamela moved back home and started living with her mother in the family house.

Pamela worked at the library and had a lover who visited her only at night . . . and never talked, only had sex.

In 1988, Mama had her fall . . . and ever since, Pamela's been taking care of her.

The best way to describe Pamela is erratic. She seems quiet and sensitive and ready to please. Some people think she's timid. If they only knew what rage bubbled inside her. If they knew the outrage she feels at the way she's treated, at the insults that she perceives are hurled upon her. She has to fight each day not to kill someone because of their incompetence or disrespect. The saving grace of her life? Order. Making order out of chaos. Of having schedules. Plans to live by. Short goals made and met.

How does all this manifest itself?

Control. When her mother finally succumbs to Pamela's structured reality, things are smooth between them. Any deviation from Pamela's way . . . and there are repercussions; repercussions we only begin to learn about at the end of the first act (a three-act structure reference indicating about thirty pages).

These biographies, remember, are just ideas that are flowing out of me. (I have left them unrewritten.) I'm riffing this character. I'm not prethinking what I'm writing here. It's free-flowing, improvised, off-the-top-of-my-head ideas. I have faith that the good ones will stick and I'll lose the ideas that ultimately aren't in sync with the evolving idea.

SASHA (Glenn Close), the younger sister, twenty-one months younger than Pamela. Blond, freckled, short hair, a strong woman, is a conceptual artist. Sasha is a lesbian. She's had a nonmonogamous partner, Julia, for years. Sasha teaches art at Cooper Union and struggles to make a living.

Sasha is happy. She's in her head more than her body.

Sasha always felt usurped by Pamela and all her crazinesses throughout their childhood. She was always told that her sister Pamela was a "genius." At the very end of this piece, she understands that "genius" was a polite version of "crazy."

Even Sasha's character biography is being taken over by Pamela.

Once Sasha went to Bennington, and found an identity of her own—she wouldn't let Pamela visit her there—she blossomed . . . got in touch with *her* genius and became the artist she always felt she was.

And it was at Bennington she had her first lover, female. She'd fucked in high school, had boyfriends, but hadn't really hooked up emotionally with anyone. Sex was easy. Nothing else was.

As a mature woman, she had little to do with the family. It always made her feel bad. She never really felt estranged, only because things were never talked about. It's all she ever knew.

Her mother and sister, cut from the same cloth, are in some kind of dance . . . they've always been . . . and it makes Sasha crazy.

Sasha and Pamela would come home for holidays. Grandma's funeral. But not much more.

Some families are close. This one wasn't.

MOM and DAD were closet crazy people. Dad was a worker. Mom didn't really work. She was a homemaker. Took care of the

house, while Dad worked. And on weekends, Dad played soft-
ball . . . once on Saturday, once on Sunday. There was the cookout.
He was one of the anonymous workers in America. He had an
army surplus store in the bad part of town. He never took any of
his family there. He was embarrassed.

NOTES

This is something I start doing right away, making notes. I write
down anything that comes up. I don't censor any ideas; you never
know what's going to spark something else.

This should be an East Coast story.

Pamela is crafts (ceramics), Sasha is arts (conceptual art).

Sasha's sometime-partner Julia has to come to the house to visit.
Worried she hasn't heard from Sasha.

Pamela remembers slights from her childhood as if they were yes-
terday or today.

Other complications that happen to sisters in house.

A worried Julia visits.

TIME PASSES

Here I go again. I've let the idea sit for a while. I've pitched it to
family and friends and everyone seems to think I'm on the right
track. It's valuable for me to get some reactions to an idea. When I
do pitch it, I inevitably riff on it and it evolves. I also get feedback
that gets me thinking of things I hadn't thought of before.

I've done character bios, made notes, mulled it over, let it season,
now here's the next crack at the story. It's now that the rewriting
begins.

My expectations for the rewrite?

To expand the story, to deepen it. I know I have to make this
smart if I want to attract major actresses. I'm waiting for that ele-
ment to come in. And, of course, it has to start getting more specific. There's no hurry. It just comes when it comes.

Here I go . . .

HOUSE OF PAIN (DRAFT TWO)

Introduce artist Glenn in her life. Vibrant. Alive. Independent. Mid-forties, a strong, blond, short-haired woman. It's a gallery opening in NYC. Glenn's conceptual art. Interesting. Weird. Mention is made of her family. They live upstate (not far enough not to come). Friend from high school asks about sister, Pamela.

Mama calls out "Pamela!" She's bedridden and looks like death warmed over. (It's only later in the scene do we realize she's tied to the bed.) Meryl has been taking care of Mama since her fall in 1988.

There was talk of Mama faking her injuries, Glenn said she was, but Meryl believed her and took care of her, in the family house, until now, when she appears to be dying.

At the doctor's suggestion, Meryl calls Glenn; it's time to come home.

Glenn comes home . . . and it's the nightmare.

She stays in her old room.

And falls into old ways.

It becomes intolerable . . .

Then Mama dies.

The funeral.

Going through things, Glenn begins finding things.

Piles of unopened, unread letters from her, other people.

Meryl denies.

Bloody rags.

Stories of Mama's craziness.

Mama's journal. That Glenn reads to Meryl.

Then Meryl attacks Glenn, knocks her out.

Glenn wakes up . . . she's strapped to the bed . . .

And Meryl is who she wants to be . . .

Who she was with Mama.

The Caretaker. In charge.

And Meryl takes care of her . . .

Feeds her . . .

Gets angry at her . . .

Tortures her.

And Glenn realizes Meryl killed their mother . . .

And is going to kill her.
Because Meryl is psychotic.
A killer . . .
She killed their father . . .
Their mother . . .
And now her.
But Glenn fights back . . .
And is about to escape, but doesn't.
And things get worse.
Much worse.
Until Glenn figures it out . . .
Tricks Meryl.
And Glenn is victorious.
And Meryl loses Big.
The End

Suddenly, I'm not feeling it.
I've lost faith in the idea.
I don't know why.
Suddenly in this form, it doesn't work.
It's over.
I'm dropping the project.
Oh, well.

NOTE: As I include this material in the book, the same exact thing has happened. I was excited when I read the first version—I hadn't read it in a couple of years—but when I read the second one, I got bored and didn't care again. I've made a copy of the first draft and will look at it again as a potential screenplay.

TIME PASSES

A couple months later. I pick up the idea again, mull it over, and read the scene lists, the character bios, the notes. I read the first draft. Really good. Read the second draft. It stinks. So, still excited by the first version, I decide to write on it a little, not do a scene list or organize, but to take advantage of my excitement and go for it.

Lo and behold, it didn't come out a screenplay.

It came out as prose, as fiction, as a story, who knows, maybe as a novel. As a storyteller, I felt the need, as never before, to get inside the characters' heads. While developing a rich psychological palette for each character, I got hooked on the dark, unspoken underpinnings of these characters.

What Are the Lessons Here?

Be flexible.

Be spontaneous.

Trust your instincts.

If I'm wrong and it doesn't happen as a novel, who cares? It's the process of doing it that's the fun.

Seven

TWO REWRITING CASE HISTORIES

STIGMATA

WHEN I ORIGINALLY WROTE *STIGMATA*, I WENT THROUGH MY usual ten or so drafts of rewriting, incorporating notes from readers, continuing research, before reaching my first draft. Finally, I sent it to my agents.

They liked the script, but I couldn't get them to move on it. They didn't send it out. I didn't understand.

We had a meeting. They said there wasn't a market for it so I left them for another smaller and not nearly as good agency. The new agent said the script was "brilliant." I was an easy lay.

One of the people my prior agency had sent the script to—as a sample of my work for a script assignment—was director Rupert Wainright. He called; we had lunch. He was very complimentary. A nice guy. I was flattered. He loved the script and wanted to run with it. No option money, but just run with it. I said fine and never heard from him again. The lunch was good. Lemon caper chicken.

NOTE: I'm asked by a lot of new writers if they should let a producer run with a script of theirs without putting up any money. My answer is yes. Embrace producers and agents who want to give you notes or run with your script. It's validation. It sets up a relationship. It's good experience. It gets you and your script out. Granted, you're not getting any option money, but think big picture. Someone's interested in your script. Make sure not to give the producer/agent an exclusive on the material. You should still be free to go elsewhere (money) with it if the occasion arises. The question is, what do you have to lose versus what do you have to gain? I think the positives outweigh the negatives.

Back to *Stigmata*. A producer named John Marsh, a quirky, smart guy who worked for a tiny production company named Chestnut Hill, read the script—another try for an assignment before I left that agency—and he loved it. He had Chestnut Hill option it.

I did three more drafts of the script with him, making it more of a horror movie before John sent out the script to production companies and studios.

A hot production company at the time, Propaganda, optioned the script. Young and hip with a background in commercials, Propaganda was run by Steve Golin, a small aggressive man, and Joni Sighvatsson, tall, thin, laid back. When I had the rewrite meeting with them, they gave me totally different notes. Polar opposites. And what made it crazy, of the seven people in the room—John Marsh and miscellaneous development people—I seemed to be the only one who noticed. One wanted it more horror. The other wanted it more religious. It made me crazy. John Marsh told me to listen to his notes exclusively and I did. The rewrite was coherent and good.

I wrote two more drafts for them, much more horror and special effects. Propaganda didn't make the film.

By now, the script had taken on shapes and colors that didn't make me terribly happy, so when their option ran out and I owned it again, I wrote two more drafts, took the best from the other scripts, and restored the parts from the original that I liked.

Next, the Pierce brothers were interested in the script. They were the sons of the ex-head of ABC Fred Pierce, who had a production company, and loved the script. They envisioned the script as an

Easter franchise picture on television. I thought they were out of their minds. But the possibility of money made me very accommodating. Of course, they said we'd have to lose the horror elements and push the religious, feel-good aspects of *Stigmata*. Less blood. More spiritual. They said it could be a holiday perennial, like *It's a Wonderful Life*. Huh? They offered me zero money for the projected rewrites, so I passed at my chance to write the new *It's a Wonderful Life*. If I'd had faith in their approach I might have made another decision.

All in all, probably six years had passed from the time I had originally thought of *Stigmata* and I was losing steam. Maybe it wasn't as good as I thought.

Then, out of the blue, Rupert called. He had pitched another project to MGM producer Frank Mancuso, who among his other credits had a father who was running the company. Mancuso passed on the project Rupert walked in with and told him he was looking for a religious horror movie. Rupert told him he had the perfect script: *Stigmata*. Mancuso read it, liked it, and three weeks later I had a deal. Out of the blue. A studio picture and a deal in the hundreds of thousands of dollars.

After twenty-three years as a screenwriter—sometimes making a great living, sometimes being literally broke—here was the jackpot. Easy street. Break open the Champagne. Hard to believe. It was as if I had been struck by lightning. And I loved it. My goal when I started being a writer more than three decades ago was to become a writer/director in Hollywood. I had just finished writing and directing a couple of low-budget movies and now I had an original screenplay going to be made by a major studio. I seemingly had reached my goals.

Headline: "MIRACLE!! SCREENWRITER FEELS GOOD!"

Then came the rewrite. I would go to Rupert's beautiful old Hollywood Hills Spanish courtyard apartment. (Steven Soderberg lived upstairs. I always had the fantasy of throwing scripts of mine up onto his balcony, he'd read them . . . the rest? History.) and we would work on the rewrite. He had lots of really good ideas and, though we did have our arguments, we did a lot of good work. He definitely had his fix and it was good. It made the script better.

The most memorable rewrite meeting we had reminded me of one of the classic *Saturday Night Live* bits. Remember the one with diners eating in a fancy restaurant and the tuxedoed waiter, Dan Ackroyd, would be gallant and polite to the diners, then go into the kitchen, where the diners would hear a knock-down drag-out shouting fight with Gilda Radner; only to have Ackroyd return, disheveled, never mentioning the fracas in the kitchen, and continue his smarmy, diner-pleasing behavior? This routine was repeated three times and was funnier each time.

Well, I lived through that with Rupert and a woman, unseen in the bedroom. Rupert and I were working in his dining room, battling about the direction of the script, then, English accent and all, he'd politely excuse himself and walk into his bedroom where he'd have a top-of-their-lungs, name-calling shouting match with the unseen woman, then return, a bit disheveled, and continue our notes meeting. This happened three or four times that day, each argument louder and more heated than the last. Each time he would return, his face would be redder. We would resume working as if nothing had happened.

Finally, Rupert cracked, found our creative conflict too much, and kicked me out of his house and off the picture. Getting home was a nightmare. I thought I'd never work in this town again. He'd steal my credit. I'd be disgraced. Time to break out the shovel and commence with my fall-back position: potato farming. A small spread somewhere. Dirt under my fingernails. No rewrite notes. Potatoes. It was a long drive home.

By the time I got there, my answering machine was blinking. It was a message from Rupert apologizing profusely and setting up another meeting. Saved!

In retrospect, as soon as the shouting matches started, I should have left. I didn't and I was off the movie.

We finished the rewrite in relative peace and then I was off the picture as if I had the plague.

The studio brought in Writer B, who—with Rupert—rounded the script into shape enough for MGM to begin production.

The Lesson to Be Learned?

I did thirty drafts and another writer did a couple more before *Stigmata* went into production. Whatever it takes. Keep plugging. From the moment the idea for that movie popped into my head, I knew it was a viable project. It took more than eight years.

A Personal Aside

There was a moment, opening night of *Stigmata,* that was truly amazing. The picture opened wide. Lots of theaters. I went with Stevie and my daughter, Jennifer, to the Galaxy Multiplex on Hollywood Boulevard, one of the bigger houses it was playing in to see how it was doing.

When we got there, what I saw took my breath away. Lines. Around the block. They had to open another theater to handle the larger-than-expected opening-night crush. It's the high point of my career so far.

THE WHISTLERS

An Italian production company, a major player in the European market, hired me to rewrite an existing script that had already gone through three drafts by the original writer. It was good money and a chance to open up a new income source because they were such an important company in Italy, so I said yes.

The cast of characters involved: the weirdly suave, chain-smoking production executive for the Italian company in Los Angeles; his inscrutable Argentinian development guy; the illusive and obtuse development guy from Rome, the constantly-telling-a-joke American producer who brought me in on the project; as well as the development person for the production company's production partner, a young woman of vague talent whose frightened eyes gave away that she was in terribly over her head.

I read the existing draft—it was truly awful—with really basic problems:

The heroine was passive, wasn't in key scenes.

The actions of the heroine didn't drive the story.

Bad writing.

At the initial meeting, the cast of characters assembled. I told them what I thought. Everyone agreed: I was brilliant and I was off and writing.

I love Hollywood.

When I handed in my draft, the trouble began. At the first notes meeting there were four different voices giving rewrite notes. The nightmare. Everyone had an idea. All different and some contradictory. It was a very difficult meeting because I felt the script (read: me) was under attack. I also didn't respect a lot of the people in the room and felt their notes weren't thought out or were poorly thought out. If I did do them, I would savage the script. I was stubborn. It was contentious. We finally agreed to the rewrite.

I was off rewriting again, doing the notes I agreed with and not doing the notes that made no sense to me. **The writer's job is to field all the notes and do the ones we agree with, the ones that are true to the story, the ones that make it better.** This sometimes gets you fired, but I believe it's what our job is. We're not supposed to sit and take notes and do them all without question. Not my style.

In this case, the cliché that a camel is a horse designed by committee is the gospel truth.

I'm sure you've experienced this: You've gone to the movies, the director's good, a major studio release, the screenwriter's famous, the stars bankable, yet the picture is a stinker. What happened? Remember the camel. A lot of powerful voices all being listened to, resulting in a mess. My bias, because I'm a writer/director, is that a single vision results in more satisfying, consistent, and coherent projects.

When I handed in the next draft of *The Whistlers,* I heard nothing for a long while. Too long a while.

My agent finally told me there'd been a personal tragedy in the Production Executive's family and he was missing in action, the

Italian company went under with all hands, and the option on the property became due and wasn't paid.

End of project.

I made some money.

There wasn't too much pain.

Eight

REWRITING FOR THE DIRECTOR

Rewriting for Rupert Wainwright, the director of Stig-mata, was an incredible learning experience for me. It was my first rewrite of a script that was getting a big studio production budget. It was green-lit with a budget of over $30 million.

It started the day after I signed my contract with MGM. Rupert and I had a meeting. He explained his vision of the movie and told me that's what the producer and MGM had bought. Then, he and the producer, Frank Mancuso, and I had a rewrite meeting with MGM, who was ponying up the money.

Rupert took the meeting. He was really good and pitched them his vision of the movie. He said I was in total agreement and we were ready to go. He was the Eight-Hundred-Pound Gorilla and he pulled it off. I said a few things in the meeting, but he was the guy and it worked. MGM gave us their blessing and we were off and running.

It was clear to me that I, as creator and writer who had already spent seven years and written something like thirty drafts, had to give the creative reins of the project over to Rupert, as director. He was the boss now and to stay on the project, I was effectively working for him. So that's what I did and, in large part, it worked.

Why Go Along with It?

Simply put: money. The longer I stay on the project, still writing away, the better chance I have of retaining my credit. The more I retain my credit, the more money I make. It's how I keep myself in fast cars and faster women.

Was I Involved with the Production?

I had a meeting with the producer one day during production, to pitch him a new project—strike while the iron's hot and all that—and we walked onto the set of *Stigmata*. They were filming a scene I hadn't written. It looked trendy and cheap and awful. Rupert walked over, saw, I suppose, the look of abject horror on my face, brusquely said hello, and went back to work. I stood there for a moment feeling like the proverbial largest fifth wheel in the world, and then fled.

What Is Considered "Writing"?

Right before *Stigmata* opened, I received a call from Rupert announcing that he was going to seek writer's credit, which he said he would almost surely get.

I said OK.

He said, "After all the work I've done it's hard to imagine I won't get it."

I said OK, and asked him how many pages or scenes or drafts he'd done.

He said none, that none of it was on paper.

I told him, "My belief is that you actually have to write something to get writer's credit."

His name never came up in the credit arbitration.

Headline: "SCREENWRITER REACHES THROUGH PHONE AND STRANGLES DIRECTOR!"

Nine

STAR REWRITES

MIKE HAMMER, PRIVATE EYE

I WAS A WRITING PRODUCER FOR THIS MASSIVELY CHEAP SYNDI-cated show starring Stacy Keach as Mike Hammer. I was working for a low-end production company which, by the way, still owes me money, but it was a paycheck and I was happy to have the job.

The process was weird. I'd work out the story with the supervising producer, Phil Saltzman, a talented veteran of series television with a résumé as long and as good as anyone in the business. After we'd break the story, we'd have it written, rewritten, then we'd run it by the two Owners of the company for notes, which were usually minimal (read: negligent), and then we put it into the production hopper.

Everything would proceed swimmingly: budget, locations, set building, casting. I'd meet with the director for production rewrites. The director in television, especially in syndication, has little power, so the rewrite meetings were easy. The reason directors are relatively powerless in series television is they usually come in for a week and a half and they direct an episode with a cast and crew, producers, and writers who've been working on the show for months. The direc-tor's job is to fit in and add within an existing creative framework.

The trouble usually began the Thursday before the Monday we started to shoot a new episode. There would be a late night meeting with Stacy and the executive producer (now a drive-time talk radio host in L.A.) after shooting. Stacy would go through the script and write in his jokes, make his changes, and cross out the things he wouldn't do or say and put in things he wanted to say or do. There was no arguing. It was by Royal Decree of the Eight-Hundred-Pound Gorilla.

The next day, I would get that hodgepodge of Stacy's notes to cobble into the script. As a rule they made little sense and weren't terribly funny, and, more often than not, brought an already dangerously cheapo script down to a truly pedestrian level.

Stacy, a really nice guy and a wonderful actor, unfortunately is not the best script doctor in the world. When I complained of the script butchery to one of the owners, he shrugged. "The price of doing business."

The show quickly went off the air.

7 LIVES XPOSED

I am presently working on the scripted reality show *7 Lives Xposed,* which stars a wonderful actress who plays herself. Like *Big Brother,* it's about seven people living in a Hollywood mansion. In our third season, the story line involved a character named Jools challenging my lead for control of the house. Over the years, while waiting for the crew to set up, she and I would talk about our lives, our careers, almost anything. I wrote some of the things she told me, her fears, her goals, into her character on the show and it freaked her out. Because she plays herself in the show, the psychological dynamic was too intense, and she had trouble with it. She was, as an actress, bringing the work all the way in and letting those feelings affect her. Realizing too late that in going for a relevant, dramatic story, I was pushing buttons with her, which wasn't productive, relevant, or nice, I pulled back, but the star's rewrite notes came in the form of her behavior: She threatened to walk off the show unless she had access to all the future scripts well in advance of production. We worked it out. She's one of my all-time favorites.

When writing about someone real in a true story, it's always important to remember the impact your words will have on them.

Ten

REWRITING SOMEONE'S LIFE

REWRITING REAL LIFE IS PRESUMPTUOUS BUT ABSOLUTELY NECessary.

It's hard. People who agree to have their lives made into movies have expectations of being immortalized something like T. E. Lawrence in *Lawrence of Arabia*.

They expect to get rich.

They don't.

They expect to be part of the process.

They're usually not.

They expect to have a voice.

They usually don't.

They expect the experience to make them feel good.

It doesn't always.

The writer's job is to take years of events and whittle them down to a hundred and five pages. It's part of the definition of the job that the writer synthesizes, abridges, alters, consolidates, and makes things up to make the script work. It makes the subjects of these movies very nervous. It also makes writers crazy knowing that the real person with their time-enhanced memories of the event will read/see this and, inevitably, be terribly disappointed in the pale depiction of their life.

Obviously it's easier after the subject's passed away, one less set of notes, but then you're dealing with spouses or lawyers dedicated to leaving an untarnished memory of their loved one.

I've worked on a bunch of projects about real people. Here are a few. . . .

IN THE BELLY OF THE BEAST

Adaptation of a Life and a Book

A script based on the true story of two-time murderer Jack Henry Abbott. Very gritty, very interesting. I told my producer/partner, who had purchased outright the rights to Abbott's book and his life, that I wanted to talk to Abbott, who was serving a life term in Attica for two murders, so I could fact check, talk about his years of imprisonment after the book was written, and, most of all, find out the missing act three of his story when he escaped and lived free for a while and of which there was no information. I didn't want to misrepresent anything in Abbott's life, but I had a dramatic piece that needed details of the truth to work.

I was excited about the opportunity to meet a murderer, to study him, see his characteristics, his tics, to hear his way of speaking, how he put words together, how his eyes saw things, to see what prison was like.

The producer said no, that once Abbott had my phone number he would keep calling me forever. It had happened to him—he had to change his number. And, if Abbott didn't like the script, he was scheduled for parole in a few years and it could be dangerous. I didn't call Abbott for information. I made up what I had to make up.

I had to adapt his book, combine it with the story of his life after the book, and the imagined "true" third act.

The most interesting part of the project was the challenge of having a two-time murderer as the main character and have the reader/viewer connect with him on an emotional level. I accomplished it by having Abbott abused by horrific prison guards for the first fifty-five pages. He became the underdog and we cared about him.

HEAR NO EVIL

An ABC Movie of the Week, Based on a True Story and Court Transcripts

The true story of a cop in San Francisco who was bombed by members of the Hell's Angels Motorcycle Club, lost his hearing, and got a hearing dog . . . and revenge. In this case, there were two sides of the story that had to be dealt with. The Hell's Angels, of whom there was more than enough research, and the cop, who, for reasons the producer never explained, was not part of the project.

The big problem was one of the producers was afraid of intervention by the Hell's Angels, so he didn't want to portray them as murderers, which they clearly were. He wanted to present a "balanced picture" of these drug-dealing menaces. He ultimately quit the project because he was afraid one night there'd be a knock at his door and it'd be the Hell's Angels with rewrite notes.

While we were in production as an ABC Movie of the Week in San Francisco, a few Hell's Angels did visit the set and tried to intimidate the crew, who would have none of it. The Angels went away, never to be heard from again.

SIDE BY SIDE—THE STORY OF THE OSMOND FAMILY

NBC Movie of the Week

I slept with Marie . . . no, I didn't, but I always wanted to write a magazine piece called "My Steamy Night with Marie Osmond." I had to write about their huge family and long career and synthesize it into seven acts for a Movie of the Week. I went out to Orem, Utah, to spend research time with the Osmonds, at their house, in the studio, doing interviews for what became an NBC Movie of the Week.

This was a case of the source material, the Osmond Family, painting only the most perfect picture of their upbringing and their lives. If they were going to be immortalized in a TV movie, they wanted to control it, so they spun their lives for me. They told me a fairy tale of faith and cooperation and love. I wanted to puke. Where was the dirt, the sickness, the bile, the perversion and mayhem?

I was clearly the wrong writer for this project. I'm about as far away from the God-fearing Mormon life of the Osmonds as you can be. In order to rewrite their lives, I had to become those characters so I knew what they would say. It was a bitch.

I did three drafts. The network—who liked the script, but not enough—brought in the infamous Writer B; in this case, a lot straighter and more God-fearing than me, and he cleaned up my mess. He was a lot more in tune with the Osmond ethos, if you can call it that, than me. The picture got made and we ended up sharing credit.

DRAGONFLY

An Original Screenplay Based on a True Story and Court Transcripts

The story of a sexually harassed New York City cop. She was run out of the police force by the venality and crudeness of her fellow cops. She won a big settlement and retired to Georgia to be a bartender. I was friends with her lawyer, who told me of the story. I thought it would make a good movie.

I interviewed the subject—a really nice Irish New Yorker—by phone, read the transcripts of her sexual harassment lawsuit, then flew to New York and interviewed her face-to-face.

Her life as she perceived it and what it actually was, based on my observations, the interviews, and court transcripts, were very different. I think, in some ways, she brought it on herself by her own provocative behavior. She didn't see it that way at all and the big question for me was, which version do I write—what she told me or what I perceived? I fell somewhere in the middle and the script, unfocused and undecided, stank. It never went anywhere. My indecision killed it. I'm not convinced there was a good movie in her particular real-life story.

HELL ON WHEELS

An Unproduced Movie of the Week for CBS Based on a True Story
A Movie of the Week script about a wheelchair marathon racer. Loved the guy, loved the script. After heated discussions with the producers, I had to hide facts about his life, which were unsympathetic but wonderfully dramatic. The script was homogenized by the producers in an attempt to do what they thought the network would buy and ultimately was so compromised it never went anywhere.

WALL OF DEATH

An Unmade Deal
When I was a kid going to local carnivals and fairs, I was fascinated by the Wall of Death, a sixteen-foot-across, ten-foot-high wooden "barrel" where daredevil drivers would seemingly defy gravity as they rode noisy motorcycles around on the inside wall. I thought a traveling Wall of Death show might be something to build a TV series around.

I tracked down a guy with a Wall of Death show and proceeded to try and make a deal with him. That's when we ran into trouble. One, he thought he was going to make a lot of money. This was his fifteen minutes of fame and he was poised to cash in big-time. He was sorely disappointed when I offered to option his story for what seemed to him some ridiculously low number under five hundred dollars. This was my money, folks, and I was willing to put in the time to write the screenplay, and when I sold it, we'd both cash in. I told him it was a long shot. Which it was. I said let's be partners.

He finally agreed, I had my lawyers prepare a contract and send it to him. He balked. He was "giving everything away and ending up with nothing." He was freaked and went away. I moved on.

About six months later, he called me. He'd thought about it and now he was ready to make the deal. I told him I was busy—I was— and the moment had passed for me. We never made a deal.

VANITY SCRIPTS

I've been hired a few times by individuals to write their stories. In each case fictionalization of their lives proved too traumatic for the project to proceed beyond first draft.

THE GALAXIANS

The True Story of a Woman Channeling Aliens from the Sixth Dimension

The real-life main character, Kim, is a woman about forty-five living in the South and has been channeling aliens for the last fifteen years. She's written a book, an alien manifesto really, consisting of the channeled material from the Galaxians. The alien message was about helping humans evolve into the Golden Age on Earth.

With a first-time producer, a longtime friend, I went to the South to interview Kim and see her channel the aliens. During all of my research interviews with her, Kim—like the Osmonds—professed never having any conflict in her life. She never had a day of doubt about suddenly receiving communications from aliens from another dimension? Her husband never questioned her sanity? She never questioned her own sanity as she communicated with extraterrestrials? Suddenly communicating with aliens caused absolutely no ripples whatsoever with her family or her job or anything? Not a day of anger or insecurity, no arguments, no angry words with her now-divorced husband? No conflict there at all? Kim said it was all amicable. Huh? I didn't get it.

THE BOTTOM LINE

Feel free to rewrite someone's life to make it work in the context of script/movie. When you do a rewrite, the goal is not to change the story of the life you're writing about but to synopsize it. The challenge is to write the character in an interesting way that shows the totality of the person in a dramatic, cinematic way. Respect who you're writing about.

Eleven

THE GALAXIANS—THREE DRAFTS

In the previous chapter I dealt with the issues involved in writing about Kim, my conflict-challenged main character. I've done a lot of rewriting on this project. A *lot*. I'm a creative problem solver and I keep rewriting *The Galaxians* in different ways. Different approaches, same subject matter and information.

Here's rewriting at the most basic level: employing different creative approaches to solving the same problem. I'm using three different drafts of this script to show three totally different creative solutions to the same problem. There are literally a myriad of creative solutions to a single problem. The fun is figuring out which is best.

But First, a Little More Background on *The Galaxians*

I was brought into *The Galaxians* as an equal partner, writer—and I hoped director—by a first-time producer. An old friend I'd known for years. She knows a lot of A-list people, but has never worked in the entertainment business per se. She's never produced a movie before, but this is her shot. She was passionate about the project and that's refreshing. She's a very bright woman and, frankly, out there—and has been for years. Quirky, eccentric, New Age, on the edge. Always interesting.

The commercial value of *The Galaxians*?

It's a *true story* about aliens making contact with humans. Of the many alien scripts and projects that are around, this one is unique because it's nonfiction. I believe there's a large audience who want to hear the straight, unvarnished, nonviolent, un-Hollywood-ized true story of aliens' contact with humans.

I made a deal with the producer to adapt the book Kim wrote about her experiences and, hopefully, direct.

After two long interviews with Kim, two channeling sessions with aliens where the producer and I got to ask them questions through Kim, I went home to write.

One of the "rules" of this project the Galaxians insisted on was to tell the truth. So, I did a draft being absolutely true to the research from Kim and the aliens. My original creative solve to this problem was to write a faux documentary script so that we didn't have conflict/drama expectations of the main character. Here's the original beginning. . . .

THE GALAXIANS

Written by Tom Lazarus

FADE IN:

BLACK SCREEN

White titles: WHAT YOU'RE ABOUT TO SEE
ACTUALLY HAPPENED

EXT. KIM'S HOUSE - DAY

PANNING OFF the pale blue sky to a few film trucks
parked in the cul-de-sac of expensive houses. A PA
with earphones smokes a cigarette on the front steps
as he talks on his cell phone.

TITLE: ATLANTA, GEORGIA - 2003

INT. KIM'S HOUSE - HANDHELD - DAY

A large two-story living room looking out over a
backyard and a pool. Spiritual art and mandalas are
everywhere. A two-camera FILM CREW moves behind their
cameras.

Their subjects: DR. KIM DANIELS forty-five, an
attractive mother of a twenty-year-old, with beauty-
parlor hair, is being wired with a tiny lavalier
microphone.

She talks with BOBBIE, about the same age, glasses,
and a little overweight, and CINDY, a few years
younger and a taut, high-energy lady. They're already
wired. They could be middle-class housewives from
anywhere in America.

                    BOBBIE
          I . . . I'm a little nervous about
          this.

                    CINDY
          I hate cameras, too.

                    BOBBY
          No, I mean this film comes out . . .
                    (concerned)
          . . . people could laugh at us.

The SOUNDMAN finishes wiring Kim, disappears behind
his mixing board, and sets levels. Kim sits between
the two women and smiles calmly.

She reaches out and the three women hold hands to
bolster themselves.

INT. KIM'S HOUSE - INTERVIEW - MOMENTS LATER - DAY

The three women look seriously into CAMERA.

                    KIM
          Hello, my name is Dr. Kim Daniels.

TITLE: DR. KIM DANIELS

                    KIM
                 (continuing)
          I live in Atlanta, Georgia, and
          I'm . . .
                    (smiling)
          . . . I'm an educator. My doctorate
          is in education.

Kim looks at Cindy, who smiles nervously.

                    CINDY
          I'm Cindy Lerner.

TITLE: CINDY LERNER

                    CINDY
                 (continuing)
          I live in Savannah, Georgia. I'm an
          artist . . .
                    (smiling self-conscious)
          . . . with a definite bias toward
          spiritual and metaphysical subject
          matter.

The two women smile and look at Bobbie.

                    BOBBIE
          My name is Bobbie Smith . . .

TITLE: <u>BOBBIE SMITH</u>

                    BOBBIE
              (continuing; proudly)
      . . . and before I retired, I was
      assistant manager in the Maintenance
      Division of Georgia Bell.

Both women look to Kim.

                     KIM
                (into CAMERA)
      We can't prove what you're about to
      see in this film is true . . .

                    CINDY
      . . . and we're not going to try to.

                     KIM
      Exactly. All we can tell you is this
      is an accurate representation of how
      I received messages from Beings who
      say they're from the sixth dimension
      and what some of that information is.

                    BOBBIE
      We witnessed a great deal of all
      this and . . .
                     (nodding)
      . . . it <u>is</u> true.

Kim smiles and nods.

                     KIM
      Though there's a tremendous amount
      of material we were not able to get
      into this movie . . .

The other two women nod.

                        KIM
                   (continuing)
           . . . we've tried to organize the
           most important information in a
           coherent and understandable fashion
           that . . .

                        CINDY
                   (interrupting)
           And we told the producers when they
           first came to us, we didn't want this
           movie to have all the guns and
           violence and the usual Hollywood
           junk . . .

                        KIM
           . . . because it didn't happen that
           way.

Bobbie nods.

                        KIM
                   (continuing)
           We feel that the people who want to
           have this information want it
           straight, just as the Galaxians told
           it to me, just as it happened.

Bobbie and Cindy nod their agreement.

                        CINDY
           The images and voices depicting what
           the Galaxians have told Kim have
           been approved by them.

Kim nods, then continues straight into CAMERA.

> KIM
> To start, we have a message from the
> Galaxians. . . .

                                        FADE TO WHITE

WHITE SCREEN

An unemotional voice of no specific gender speaks
slightly faster than normal human pace.

> GALAXIAN VOICE
> We, the Galaxians, are pleased to
> make your acquaintance. We thank you
> for the opportunity to serve you. We
> salute you for the journey on which
> you are about to embark.

A red three-fingered Galaxian "hand" print is laid on
the white screen leaving the distinctive logo of the
film.

MAIN TITLES

THE GALAXIANS

FADE IN:

EXT. UNIVERSITY OF GEORGIA - DAY

The sunny campus is busy with students between
classes.

TITLE: 1990

EXT. TECHNICAL - VOCATIONAL COUNSELING CENTER - DAY -
SPLIT SCREEN

Kim walks across into the modern building.

INT. KIM'S HOUSE - INTERVIEW - DAY - SPLIT SCREEN

Kim, thirteen years later, alone in the white-flowered
tile kitchen, talks to CAMERA.

>   KIM
>   I've had a psychic streak all my
>   life. Any number of times I've felt
>   pain that friends of mine were
>   feeling. An old friend from college,
>   Stephanie, had a root canal and my
>   tooth hurt all day. Same tooth. My
>   husband, Robert, pulled his back at
>   work . . . I felt the pain before he
>   told me about it. I didn't know who
>   it was, but I knew someone I was
>   empathetic with was hurting. So,
>   when this Galaxian thing happened,
>   I'd been kind of . . .
>   (smiling)
>   . . . "warming up."

INT. COUNSELING CENTER HALLWAY - DAY

Kim walks down the highly polished linoleum floor and
enters a room at the end of the hall.

INT. COUNSELING ROOM - DAY

Large, institutional, with three doors, a number of
Formica tables with desk chairs around them.

A bulletin board lists employment opportunities, counseling seminars, students looking for roommates.

Kim checks her watch—apparently her appointment is late—then sits and spreads out her work.

A couple of files. A fresh yellow pad and a cheap ballpoint pen. She opens a file to a stack of sample submission letters and begins reading.

INT. COUNSELING ROOM - DAY - SPLIT SCREEN

ANOTHER ANGLE of KIM reading.

INT. KIM'S HOUSE - INTERVIEW - CONT'D. - DAY - SPLIT SCREEN

Kim continues to CAMERA.

>   KIM
>   It was unusual for me not to have a
>   line of people waiting to see me. I
>   counsel students and faculty on
>   career planning. But I always brought
>   work to do, just in case. Then, a
>   couple of minutes later . . .
>   (taking a deep breath, then smiling)
>   . . . it happened. . . .

INT. COUNSELING ROOM - DAY

Kim looks at another submission letter.

The yellow pad is still blank.

The pen lies beside it.

Kim is reading intently.

                    GALAXIAN VOICE
          Pick up the pen.

Kim looks up and turns to see who spoke.

No one there.

Kim turns the other way.

No one there either.

Weird.

Kim resumes reading. After a few moments . . .

                    GALAXIAN VOICE
                      (continuing)
          Pick up the pen.

Again, Kim looks around.

Still no one.

Kim looks down at the pen . . .

. . . next to the pad . . .

. . . and, after a moment, she shrugs, then picks
it up.

Hefts it . . . then moves it over the pad . . .

. . . and touches the tip to the paper . . .

. . . and waits.

OK, now what?

INT. KIM'S HOUSE - INTERVIEW - DAY - SPLIT SCREEN

Kim talks to CAMERA.

> KIM
> I didn't know what was going on. I
> had no idea where that voice came
> from.

INT. COUNSELING ROOM - DAY - SPLIT SCREEN

The tip of the pen resting on the yellow of the
paper.

INT. KIM'S HOUSE - INTERVIEW - DAY - SPLIT SCREEN -
CONT'D.

Kim continues to CAMERA.

> KIM
> So I just sat there . . . it must've
> been for two or three minutes . . .
> waiting. It was very odd . . . I
> kept waiting for something else to
> happen. I mean I felt something was
> going to happen. I didn't know what
> and I didn't know when, but I could
> feel something. Then, when nothing
> happened . . . I was thinking maybe
> I didn't hear it . . . or maybe I
> had daydreamed it or
> something. . . .

INT. COUNSELING ROOM - DAY

The tip of the pen jerks across the paper!

Kim is shocked.

Her hand is awkwardly moved across the pad.

Ink being laid onto paper.

The pen moving across the paper.

Kim's clearly not in control of her hand.

The pen moves slowly along the paper.

Arcing . . .

Purposeful.

An incredulous Kim watches.

The pen lifts up . . . starts again. . . .

Kim watches . . . fascinated. . . .

As her hand slowly, awkwardly continues writing.

Her hand starts a third time. . . .

Slowly . . . but constant.

INT. COUNSELING ROOM - DAY - SPLIT SCREEN

The tip of the pen moving on the paper.

INT. KIM'S HOUSE - INTERVIEW - DAY - SPLIT SCREEN

Kim talks to CAMERA.

                              KIM
            I wasn't scared . . . I mean at first
            I couldn't believe it. Something was
            moving my hand. I wasn't in control.
            At that point in my life, I'd never
            heard of automatic writing or
            channeling or any of that.

INT. COUNSELING ROOM - DAY

Kim's hand arcs on the paper, then stops.

Kim waits.

Nothing.

It's over. She can feel it.

Kim lifts up the pen, and lays it down next to the pad.

She studies the marks on the pad.

There are four of them. Crude shaky doodles.

Kim shakes her head. Baffling.

EXT. KIM'S HOUSE - NIGHT

Most of the lights are out in the earthen adobe-style
house. The stars are bright overhead.

                         KIM'S VOICE
                          (finishing)
             . . . and then it stopped.

INT. GEORGIA HOUSE - BEDROOM - NIGHT

ROBERT, Kim's husband, a burly man with glasses, is in
his underwear replacing his computer's motherboard. He
looks OFF CAMERA toward the bathroom.

                    ROBERT
         And then?

                    KIM'S VOICE
              (continuing from the bathroom)
          My students came in . . . and I did
          my counseling. It was over.

                    ROBERT
          You bring home the paper?

Kim, her hair up in huge pink curlers, dressed in a
modest nightgown, enters and moves to her crowded-
with-makeup dresser, opens her purse, and takes out
the now folded yellow piece of paper and walks it
over to Robert.

She sits on the bed as he unfolds and looks at it.
Rather than look at it the way Kim wrote it, he
turns it upside down . . .

                    ROBERT
              (continuing; reading)
          "G'day."

                         KIM
          What?!

He shows it to her.

                    ROBERT
          It says "G'day."

Kim looks at it. It does kind of look like "G'day."

> ROBERT
> (continuing)
> G'day. Perfect.

> KIM
> (after a beat)
> What is going on?

> ROBERT
> Beats me. It's wild. Don't worry
> about it.

He goes back to his computer.

> KIM
> Easy for you to say.

Robert LAUGHS.

> ROBERT
> OK, worry about it.

Kim climbs in bed. Robert takes off his glasses and
turns out the light.

In the moonlight, they kiss, then rustle around
readying for sleep. After they're settled . . .

> ROBERT
> (continuing)
> 'Night.

                    KIM
          It's the most amazing thing that's
          ever happened to me.
                    (blown away)
          Something else was controlling my
          hand.

Robert slides over next to her.

                    ROBERT
                    (playful)
          Why don't you control your hand over
          here?

And they both LAUGH . . . and he takes her in his
arms.

INT. KIM'S HOUSE - INTERVIEW - DAY

Kim shakes her head and talks to CAMERA.

                    KIM
          What had happened really stuck with
          me. I thought about it all day . . .
          and now, when I think about it, I
          instinctively didn't tell anyone
          about it. The next night, after
          work, I took out the same pad and
          pen. . . .

INT. KIM'S HOUSE - DINING ROOM - NIGHT

The same yellow pad and the same pen on the dining
room table crowded with mail, magazines, and
newspapers.

Kim circles the table . . .

. . . nervously . . . suddenly undecided, unsure . . .

. . . then she sits . . . takes a deep breath and picks up the pen, puts it on the paper . . . and waits.

And waits.

And waits . . .

. . . until just as she's about to give up, the pen finally lurches across the paper.

Kim lights up.

The pen moves on the paper.

A fascinated Kim watches the pen on the paper and smiles.

Her hand moves a little faster. . . .

A little more coherently.

"Good day."

Kim shrugs self-consciously. . . .

                    KIM
          Good day to you.

EXT. KIM'S HOUSE - BACKYARD - NIGHT - SPLIT SCREEN

Robert stops stripping an old oak table and looks curiously into the house.

INT. KIM'S DINING ROOM - NIGHT - SPLIT SCREEN

In jeans and a blouse, Kim at the counter . . .
automatic writing. She's writing much quicker. She
still has that distinct posture that someone else is
controlling her hand. She stops, flexes her cramping
hand, then continues.

EXT. UNIVERSITY COUNSELING CENTER - DAY

Students sitting on the steps.

INT. COUNSELING CENTER - DAY

Kim in front of her clients. One is standing at his
seat.

                    CLIENT
                   (midrap)
          . . . then she asked me if I was
          qualified on those programs and I
          froze.

Kim's clearly not listening. Her eyes are on the
yellow pad and pen in front of her.

                    CLIENT
                  (continuing)
          I felt like, like a doofus.

                    KIM
          Okay, thanks. I have to stop early
          today. Sorry.

And Kim quickly packs her pad and pen in her book bag
and exits.

The students look around at each other in disbelief.

INT. ROBERT'S CONDO - INTERVIEW - NIGHT

Robert, ten years heavier and grayer, now with a crew cut, lives in a computer-filled two-bedroom place with lots of sun. Robert talks to CAMERA.

                    ROBERT
          Kim was totally focused on doing the
          automatic writing.
                    (suddenly diplomatic)
          I mean . . . she did have that
          traffic accident a little before all
          this stuff happened.
                    (shrugging)
          I don't know if they're
          connected . . . but to me . . .

He doesn't finish.

EXT. KIM'S HOUSE - NIGHT

Few lights on.

                    KIM'S VOICE
          I let my session go early and went
          up on the Internet.

INT. KIM'S BATHROOM - NIGHT

Kim brushing out her hair.

                    KIM
          (continuing, into the bedroom)
     What I'm doing is called automatic
     writing. There's documented cases of
     it, anecdotal mostly, but still very
     impressive.

No response.

                    KIM
               (continuing)
          Robert?

No answer. Kim smiles and turns out the light.

INT. KIM'S BEDROOM - NIGHT

Robert is asleep on his side of the bed. Kim smiles,
walks over, takes off his glasses, turns off his
reading light, then climbs into bed, turns out her
light, and settles back to sleep.

But Kim's eyes blink in the near darkness.

After a few moments, she turns the light back on,
checks to see if she's disturbed Robert—she hasn't—
then picks up her yellow pad and a pencil off the
night table.

She puts the pencil to the paper . . . and instantly
she's writing . . .

. . . quickly, surely . . . legibly.

Some other force controlling her hand.

INT. KIM'S BEDROOM - NIGHT - SPLIT SCREEN

Kim's fascinated.

INSERT ON PAPER - SPLIT SCREEN

As Kim writes We, the Galaxians, thank you for having an open mind.

INT. KIM'S BEDROOM - NIGHT

Kim drops the pencil. She can't believe it. Writing.
Clear and legible. She reads it and mouths the words.
Now, for the first time, she's very freaked out.

INT. KIM'S HOUSE - INTERVIEW - DAY

Kim talks to CAMERA.

                    KIM
          I was raised Catholic, but I have an
          open mind. I've always been
          intellectually curious. The whole
          automatic writing business . . . I
          didn't know what was going on . . .
          but I really became hooked. I'd come
          home at night, eat dinner fast, then
          pick up a pen or pencil and I was
          off to the races. One night after a
          couple of weeks, the Galaxians asked
          me to get some crystals. . . .
                    (smiling and shrugging)
          So . . .

INT. KIM'S DINING ROOM - NIGHT

Kim sits with her pad, pen, and now a number of
small, beautiful crystals and sparkling geodes.

Kim takes a sip of her tea and picks up the pen.
Instantly she's writing . . . as fast as she ever has.

TIGHT ON KIM - SPLIT SCREEN

Kim is fascinated.

ON THE PAD - SPLIT SCREEN

<u>We, the Galaxians, are from a planet named Galaxia.</u>
<u>We are riding on a starship situated southeast of</u>
<u>Atlanta.</u>

INT. KIM'S DINING ROOM - NIGHT - CONTINUED

Robert passes on his way to the kitchen and sees the
startled Kim, her eyes blinking with thought, her pen
flying across the pad.

She writes a question.

<u>Where is Galaxia?</u>

Kim waits a second, then writes.

<u>We are from the Sixth Dimension.</u>

Again, Kim is startled.

Her hand writes of its own accord again.

Robert walks back through with his cold beer.

ON THE PAD - SPLIT SCREEN

<u>We have been selected to answer your questions</u>
<u>tonight.</u>

My Producer Didn't Like the Draft

She was confused by the format. The different times of the interviews didn't work for her. She was expecting what she described as a *Star Wars* kind of epic. With the same kind of big commercial beats. She explained to me, as if I were a neophyte in the business, why and how people connect to movies. She said *The Galaxians* needed to be an adventure with a hero audiences could related to. We had to *see* the aliens. We had to show them in artists' renderings. And lots more.

I asked what happened to adapting Kim's book, which was the source of the Galaxians' message. What happened to telling only the truth?

The producer said it was a matter of interpretation. Oh.

We had more meetings.

The producer was all over the place.

Now the movie had to be about how women are revered in Bali.

Then it changed. Now it had to be about the effect of Sixth-Dimension thinking on present society.

Then it had to be about a CIA agent's paranormal-powered daughter.

We both did agree that Kim's story, the straight truth, wasn't enough.

I brought into the mix that the aliens would answer the issues that are on our core audience's mind: What happened at Roswell? What is the story behind crop circles? More about other aliens. This material would appeal to UFO/conspiracy fans.

The original project had started as an adaptation of sorts of Kim's book, recounting her experiences channeling the aliens. Now the script was evolving as it was being rewritten.

After more tumultuous meetings, the producer and I agreed to a new creative approach—a page one rewrite.

I wrote two drafts trying to make this approach work, but it stank.

At home in Georgia, the actual Kim continued channeling the Galaxians, who kept saying the script had to be a "masterpiece" or it would be a total failure. Thanks. The producer kept talking about the script transforming people. Pretty tall order. Then I moved on and tried something else. Something more normal with Kim as main character. I started the story in a different place, with a set-up of Kim's paranormalness; put in chapter headings, put in Robert's skepticism. I jettisoned Bobbie and Cindy.

I wrote my brains out, working on the fourth draft, and came up with this. . . .

THE GALAXIANS

Screenplay by Tom Lazarus

```
FADE IN:

BLACK SCREEN

White titles:  WHAT YOU ARE ABOUT TO SEE
               IS A WOMAN'S TRUE ADVENTURE
               WITH EXTRATERRESTRIALS

                                    DISSOLVE TO:

EXT. ATLANTA AIRPORT - DAY

An airplane touches down with a SCREECH of tires.

Title: ATLANTA, GEORGIA

Cars enter the airport traffic to let off departing
passengers.

BLACK SCREEN

White titles:          IT BEGINS

August 14, 1982

EXT. ATLANTA AIRPORT - DAY
```

A dusty Oldsmobile, a dent in the front fender, slows down at the American Airlines terminal.

Inside the car, ROBERT DANIELS, burly, with glasses, a bulging attaché case, leans over, kisses the driver, DR. KIM DANIELS, thirty-five, an attractive woman with beauty-parlor hair, wearing a Falcons T-shirt. Robert climbs out. He waves as the Oldsmobile drives off.

In the backseat, ROBERT, JR., fifteen, long hair below his shoulders, is listening to his Walkman and not paying any attention.

EXT. ATLANTA AIRPORT APPROACH - DAY

The Oldsmobile moves away from the airport.

EXT. INTERSECTION - DAY

The Oldsmobile slows at the red light, then stops.

A green four-door ROARS right at them from behind!

The car CRASHES into the rear of Kim's car with a HUGE METALLIC SLAM!

Kim and Robert, Jr., are jarred traumatically.

The passenger in the green car flies out of the car and sprawls across the road.

Smoke!

Bent metal!

Shattered glass!

Frightening.

An eerie post-accident silence . . .

Then MOANS and CRIES.

INT. GEORGIA HOUSE - LIVING ROOM - DAY

Kim talks to CAMERA.

>   KIM
>   Thank God, we weren't seriously hurt
>   or killed. Robert, Jr., was fine. I
>   had a bad neck for a couple of
>   years. I needed a ton of physical
>   therapy . . . but, most importantly,
>   I believe it cracked open my etheric
>   shell and changed my life
>   forever. . . .

EXT. GEORGIA HOUSE - NIGHT

The white stucco house in the moonlight.

BLACK SCREEN

White titles:

A CHANGE

FEBRUARY 1984

INT. GEORGIA BEDROOM - NIGHT

Kim bolts upright in bed. . . .

Her eyes blink . . . registering.

Robert turns over.

> ROBERT
> What?

> KIM
> It's my niece Tracy, there's hearts
> and flowers all around her . . .
>> (shaking her head)
> . . . I saw it so clear . . . so
> clear.

> ROBERT
> You were dreaming.

> KIM
> She was talking to me . . . she said
> she was all right.

Robert turns over again.

> ROBERT
> Just go back to bed.

Kim lies back down.

EXT. GEORGIA HOUSE - DAY

The sun is bright.

INT. GEORGIA KITCHEN - DAY

Kim fixing breakfast. Robert pouring coffee.

> ROBERT
> Any more dreams?

                         KIM
          No, but that one was . . .

The phone RINGS. Kim reaches over, picks up the phone.

                         KIM
                     (continuing)
          Hello . . .
                     (listening)
          What?

Kim's tone concerns Robert.

                         KIM
                     (continuing)
          When? Oh, my God . . .

She holds her hand over the phone.

                         KIM
                     (continuing)
          Tracy died last night.

Robert can't believe it.

                         KIM
                     (continuing)
          How's Margie?
                     (darkening)
          I can imagine. We'll come up.
                     (listening)
          Of course.

EXT. SACRAMENTO, CALIFORNIA - DAY

A modest house in a nice neighborhood. Robert is
outside with Tracy's father, GEORGE, who's smoking a
cigarette.

Titles: <u>THE NEXT DAY</u>

INT. MODEST HOUSE - LIVING ROOM - DAY

Kim sits with MARGIE, a woman in tears, and DEBORAH, her mother.

> KIM
>
> Ever since my car accident, it's like I am very empathetic. My friend Lauri had a toothache . . . I felt it. Robert pulled his back at work . . . I felt it.

> MARGIE
> (not understanding)
>
> I just want to know what happened . . . she just ran in a marathon . . . nothing was wrong . . . I don't understand. What happened to her?

Kim puts her hand on Margie's.

> KIM
>
> I think Tracy reached out for me last night.

Margie can't believe it.

> KIM
> (continuing)
>
> I think I can communicate with her . . . maybe she can tell you what happened.

Margie thinks for a second, then turns to her mother.

                          DEBORAH
          I think you should.

Margie turns to Kim and nods.

Kim takes a deep breath and closes her eyes. After a
few moments . . .

                            KIM
          I see hearts and flowers.

Margie gasps. Deborah crosses herself.

                          MARGIE
                    (barely audible)
          She always doodled hearts and
          flowers . . . her room's filled with
          them.

Kim "listens" for a moment, then . . .

                            KIM
          Tracy says she loves you.

Tears well out of Margie's eyes.

                            KIM
                    (continuing)
          And she's all right.

She smiles. Margie wipes away the tears. . . .

>   KIM
>   (continuing)
>   She said it was her time to go . . .
>   her lungs filled up with fluid and she
>   crossed over . . . and she's happier
>   than she's ever been.

Margie, for the first time, smiles and hugs Kim
thankfully.

BLACK SCREEN

White titles:

FIRST CONTACT

AUGUST 14, 1984

EXT. TECHNICAL - VOCATIONAL INSTITUTE - DAY

The bright sun of the prestigious campus busy with
students between classes.

EXT. CAREER CENTER - DAY

In a conservative business suit, carrying a book bag,
Kim walks through the dappled sunlight into the
modern building.

INT. CAREER CENTER - HALLWAY - DAY

Kim heads down the highly polished linoleum floor and
enters the counseling room at the end of the hall.

INT. COUNSELING ROOM - DAY

A bulletin board lists employment opportunities, counseling seminars, students looking for roommates, used textbooks for sale.

Kim checks her watch—apparently her appointments are late—then sits at the wood conference table, pulls files and papers out of the book bag and spreads out her work, a couple of files, a fresh yellow pad, a cheap ballpoint pen.

She opens a file to a stack of sample submission letters and begins reading.

The yellow pad is still blank.

The pen lies beside it.

Kim reading intently. After a few moments . . .

                    GENDERLESS VOICE
          Pick up a pen.

Kim looks up and turns to see who spoke.

No one there.

Kim turns the other way.

No one there either.

Weird.

Kim resumes reading.

Another few beats . . .

                         GENERLESS VOICE
                   (continuing; a bit more assertive)
                      Pick up a pen.

Again, Kim looks around.

Still no one.

Kim looks down at the pen . . .

    . . . next to the pad . . .

    . . . and, after a moment, she picks it up.

Hefts it . . .

    . . . then moves it over the pad . . .

    . . . and touches the tip to the paper . . .

    . . . and waits.

Okay, now what?

The tip of the pen resting on the yellow of the
paper.

Waiting.

Kim looks around.

She shrugs.

Still waiting . . . then:

The tip of the pen quivers!

Kim can't believe it.

Her hand _is moved_ awkwardly across the pad.

Ink being laid onto paper.

The pen moving across the paper.

Kim's clearly not in control of her hand.

The pen moves very slowly along the paper.

Arcing . . .

Purposeful.

An incredulous Kim watches.

The pen lifts up . . .

. . . starts again.

Kim watches . . . fascinated.

As her hand slowly, awkwardly continues writing.

Her hand starts a third time. . . .

Slowly . . . but constant.

Kim's hand arcs on the paper, then stops.

She waits.

Nothing.

It's over. She can feel it.

Kim takes a deep breath.

She lifts up the pen and lays it down next to the pad. She studies the marks on the pad.

There are four of them. Crude shaky doodles.

Kim is totally baffled.

EXT. GEORGIA HOUSE - NIGHT

The stars bright overhead. Most of the lights are out in the white stucco house.

INT. GEORGIA HOUSE - BEDROOM - NIGHT

Robert is in his underwear looking through the newspaper for the sports section. He looks OFF CAMERA toward the bathroom.

                    ROBERT
          And then?

                    KIM'S VOICE
                (from the bathroom)
          It was over. I put the pen down and
          my students came in . . . and I did
          my counseling. That was it.

                    ROBERT
          You bring home the paper?

Her hair up in huge pink curlers, wearing a modest nightgown, Kim enters and moves to her crowded-with-makeup dresser, opens her purse and takes out the now folded yellow piece of paper and walks it over to Robert.

KIM

It was the damnedest thing that ever
happened to me, I can tell you that.

She sits on the bed as he unfolds and looks at it.
Rather than look at it the way Kim wrote it, he turns
it upside down. . . .

ROBERT
(reading)

"G'day."

KIM

What?!

He shows her to it.

KIM
(continuing)

It says "G'day."

Kim looks at it. It does kind of look like "G'day."
Robert LAUGHS.

ROBERT

G'day. Perfect.

KIM
(after a beat)

What is going on?

ROBERT

Beats me. It's wild.

A worried Kim climbs in bed.

Unconcerned, Robert takes off his glasses and turns out the light.

In the moonlight, they kiss good night, then rustle around readying for sleep.

After they're settled . . .

> KIM'S VOICE
> Something, not me, was controlling
> my hand.

After a beat . . .

> ROBERT
> Don't worry about it. 'Night.

She looks over at Robert, but his eyes are closed. She settles back on her pillow . . . her eyes blink with thought . . . and possibilities. . . .

After a few moments as Robert's breathing evens . . .

> KIM
> (whispering)
> Honey? . . .

No answer.

She carefully climbs out of bed, pulls her robe around her, and heads out.

INT. GEORGIA HOUSE - DINING ROOM - NIGHT

The light clicks on.

The same yellow pad and the same pen on the dining room table crowded with mail, magazines, and the newspaper.

Kim enters and circles the table . . .

. . . nervously . . . suddenly undecided, unsure . . .

. . . then she sits . . .

. . . takes a deep breath and picks up the pen,

puts it on the paper . . . and waits.

And waits.

And waits . . . and nothing happens . . .

. . . until, just as she's about to give up, the pen finally lurches across the paper.

Kim drops the pen, then breaks into an excited smile.

She looks at the pen, then after a moment cautiously picks it up.

Instantly, the pen is moved on the paper.

A fascinated Kim watches the pen on the paper and her smile becomes a grin.

Her hand moves a little faster . . .

. . . a little more coherently.

"Good day."

Kim shrugs self-consciously. . . .

                    KIM
          OK, good day to you.

BLACK SCREEN

White titles:

THEY IDENTIFY THEMSELVES

October 1, 1986

EXT. GEORGIA HOUSE - BACKYARD - DAY

A beautiful Southern sky.

Robert is stripping an old oak table. He stops and
looks curiously into the house.

INT. GEORGIA DINING ROOM - DAY

A large stack of already-written-on pages. In jeans
and a blouse, Kim at the counter writing with her pen
on the yellow pad.

She's writing much quicker.

She still has the distinct posture that someone or
something else is controlling her hand.

She stops, flexes her cramping hand, then continues.

Robert enters and watches for a few seconds,
then . . .

                    ROBERT
          You know, what you're doing is
          called automatic writing.

Intrigued, she turns to him.

He smiles.

                    ROBERT
                  (continuing)
          I researched it.

She smiles.

                    KIM
          I love you.

He smiles . . . and continues.

                    ROBERT
          There are any number of cases of it,
          anecdotal mostly, not real scientific.

                    KIM
          Whatever it is . . . I'm getting a
          lot better at it.

                    ROBERT
          I know.

And he exits.

After a moment, Kim takes a deep breath, sits . . .
puts the pen to the paper . . . and instantly she's
writing faster than ever . . .

. . . quickly, surely . . . legibly.

INSERT ON PAPER

As Kim writes <u>We, the Galaxians, thank you for having</u>
<u>an open mind.</u>

Kim can't believe it.

Writing. Clear and legible.

She reads it and mouths the words.

Fascinating.

INT. GEORGIA DINING ROOM - DAY

Kim automatic writing quickly . . .

<u>We want you to put crystals around the area you commu-</u>
<u>nicate with us. This will facilitate our communication.</u>

Kim smiles.

EXT. GEORGIA HOUSE - BACKYARD - DAY

Kim talks to CAMERA.

                    KIM
          I'm an educator. My doctorate is in
          education and despite all that, I'm
          having a difficult time understanding
          exactly what's happening to me.
                    (smiling)
          All I know is, I'm hooked. Who or
          what are the Galaxians?

BLACK SCREEN

White titles:

POWERING UP

November 13, 1986

INT. GEORGIA LIVING ROOM - NIGHT

Next to a stack of clean, half-folded laundry, Kim
sits with her pad, pen, and now a number of small,
beautiful crystals and sparkling geodes.

>   ROBERT'S VOICE
>   What's with the crystals?

He enters and moves to the crystals and picks one up.

>   KIM
>   The Galaxians asked me to get some
>   crystals to enhance the strength of
>   their communications.

>   ROBERT
>   (skeptical)
>   Okay.

He puts down the crystal and exits.

Kim takes a sip of her tea, touches the crystals with
her other hand, then picks up the pen.

Instantly she's writing . . .

. . . as fast as she ever has.

Kim's amazed.

Robert looks in from the kitchen and sees Kim, her pen flying across the pad.

We are from the Sixth Dimension.

Again, Kim's startled.

Her hand writes of its own accord.

She's totally intrigued.

ON THE PAD

We, the Galaxians, are from a planet in the Bootes constellation named Galaxia. It is the brightest star off the end of the handle of what you call the Big Dipper. As we communicate with you, we are riding on a starship situated southeast of Atlanta.

Kim puts the pen down on the pad, breaks into an intrigued smile and walks away from the table.

INT. GEORGIA BEDROOM - NIGHT

Robert looks up to see Kim walking into the backyard.

EXT. GEORGIA BACKYARD - NIGHT

Kim looking up at the top of the house and the stars above.

No starship.

KIM'S POV

The bright star off the handle of the Big Dipper.

Catching her breath, Kim smiles.

The light of Galaxia is bright.

                    ROBERT'S VOICE
          Are you all right?

Robert joins her.

                    KIM
          This is the most . . . incredible
          thing. . . .

She flexes her tired hands. . . .

                    ROBERT
          I'm getting you a computer.

                    KIM
          But . . .

Robert shakes his head.

                    ROBERT
          I'm doing it. End of subject.

Kim smiles affectionately.

I Was in Trouble

I still believed in the project as a commercial enterprise, but nobody
liked this draft either.

The producer was disappointed. It wasn't a masterpiece.

I explained that screenwriting is a process and that this was par
for the course.

Kim was outraged. She felt I was portraying her as a "peasant." I think it must have been the one or two scenes that hinted at a sex life for her and her husband.

And even the Galaxians weighed in on the script.

Kim channeled their script notes.

Here they are. . . .

THE GALAXIANS' CRITIQUE OF THE FIRST DRAFT OF THE SCRIPT

On behalf of the higher consciousnesses involved in the motion picture project you have been working on, I, Eulonia, offer our salutations and good wishes from our starship presently in the sky above where you are receiving this transmission.

Our discussions today will outline for you the consensus view of the panel of the most creative and thoughtful minds in our world that have addressed the screenplay you have produced. Much of what you have created, though well crafted and well meaning and coming from a place of love within you all, unfortunately doesn't reach the level of excellence needed for this project to have a transformational effect on the hearts and minds of the millions of people who are its projected audience. We believe that the creative forces you are gathering to generate this successful motion picture are at a disadvantage, for they're not taking advantage of the creative tools we recommend to ensure the script reaches the potential it surely must reach to be successful and be the masterpiece we all envision. Our future masterpiece must utilize the creative powers of crystals that are indigenous in your environment and of the inspirational power of geometric shapes to focus your creative processes so that you can put aside the stereotypical thought patterns that are so familiar and that you are used to generating, and create combinations of words and images that will reach the receptive audience that is waiting for our masterpiece to transform them. Please be clear how important the synchronous harmonies and powers of the crystal and geometric designs are for maximum creativity. Do not utilize these tools at your disposal and it is tantamount to failing before you begin.

Before we are specific as to script notes for you, we do want to reiterate to you, the creative team, that honesty is the ultimate and only path this project can take. We remind you, the creators, of this golden light of a script, that any time you present material, images, or words that aren't the absolute truth, that aren't a reflection of the white light of goodness and purity, this project will be sabotaged beyond saving. The truth is the truth. Write falsehoods, even once, even in part, and our whole project will be terminally poisoned. The white light of truth must shine brightly on this masterpiece or all will be lost and all of our efforts will be for naught. This masterpiece will be a masterpiece like none other in the recorded history of planet Earth. It will employ revolutionary and radical ways to communicate to viewers on a deeper and more meaningful level than ever realized before. It will change the world.

This Cinema of Truth will be the film by which all future films will be measured. This will be the lightning rod that changes the creative environment in your world, for it will encourage other brave creators to step forth and express their true creativity bathed in the golden light of truth and free of greed and narcissism.

Only positive, golden characters should be used as the conveyors of knowledge. Rather than focusing on the false and negative dramatic elements that are replete in your present effort, we urge you to portray people who are living the white light life of the Golden Age that is to come. It is those people, those citizens of the potential future who know the Golden Path, who must be the messengers on our journey to Enlightenment.

Unfortunately, your present approach does not satisfy any of these criteria and we are convinced that unless you abandon what you've started and approach the material with more reverence toward Kim, treating her with the awe and respect fitting for a person between worlds as she is, the project we are all counting on to pave the way for the entrance into the Golden Age and the Hall of Truth we are hoping to help you attain will fail.

An example of this highest level of creativity we are presenting to you is the motion picture masterpiece *Pretty Woman*. This successful product of the highest creative minds is an example of superior craftsmanship which allows it to be successful in its intent on reaching into people's hearts and affecting change. In what we have read so far of your script, the craftsmanship and positive point of view is not present. If you portray characters, as you have, embroiled in endless cycles of unhappiness and selfishness, then all will be lost and our masterpiece will be stillborn. Because of the importance of the positive energy of the future, we strongly suggest not presenting any scenes that depict the past, but only have scenes colored by the glow of the Golden Age.

So, creators, I, Eulonia, tell you the work has just begun, knowing that what you have done so far has been practice and that now you are on the right path as long as you keep focused on our truthful goal. If you are successful in your creative endeavors you will experience yourselves walking the path of the Golden future.

I love Hollywood!

I had more meetings with the producer. She would read me passages of the alien rewrite notes and try and find meaning.

The Galaxians said I needed my brain "reconfigured" if I was to successfully write the script.

At the end of my rope, I agreed. It would take a few months.

I was struggling. I felt writing only the truth was really hindering me. I tried a couple rewrites on the last approach. But I was unconvinced. And if I'm not convinced, I don't write.

So I took a step back. Wrote something else. Cleaned out my head, then came back to it. I was being urged by my writer friends to drop this project like a hot rock: rookie producer, odd main character, material we've seen a million times, move on.

Then I had an idea. I came up with an *Adaptation*-like solution. Rewrite the script about the struggle I've been having writing the script. It was still the truth and it had more drama and conflict than any part of the story and it reflected some of the humor that was, at this point, inescapable. So I rewrote the script again, for the fifth time.

THE GALAXIANS

Screenplay by Tom Lazarus

FADE IN:

BLACK SCREEN

White titles:

A TRUE STORY
Based on tapes and transcripts
of real events and the channeling
of Dr. Kim Daniels

INT. HOLLYWOOD SOUND STAGE - DAY

A busty, naked actress on her cell phone as she has
body makeup applied by two Makeup People.

Gaffers and Grips tweak lights and reflectors as they
set up for the next shot.

Prop guys prepare the set to look like a party room.

MASON, the director, handsome, lean, forty, talks on
his cell phone. He sits on a director's chair with
DIRECTOR on the back.

> MASON
> (into the phone)
> Toni, I'm always looking for ideas
> for scripts.

As Mason listens, the Makeup Key parades the naked
actress in front of him. Mason motions for her to
spin around. She does. He nods his approval.

                    MASON
                (continuing)
        Thanks.
                (into the phone)
        Send me the book, I'll read it,
        we'll meet for sushi.
                (listening)
        Thanks. I'm up for it.

Mason gets up and walks out onto the set.

                    MASON
                (continuing)
        More shadows.
                (unhappily, under his breath)
        Less silicone.

INT. SUSHI RESTAURANT - NIGHT

A Japanese Waitress brings a platter of sushi and
puts it down on the table between Mason, in a
baseball cap and sweatshirt, and TONI, a perfectly
madeup woman Mason's age, in heels and a Sgt.
Pepper's blazer with epaulets and medals.

                    MASON
                (to the Waitress)
        Thanks a lot.

Toni smiles.

Mason reaches into his briefcase, pulls out a THE
GALAXIANS paperback and hands it to her.

                    TONI
                (excited)
        So?

                    MASON
     I think there's a huge audience out
     there for a true story of a woman
     channeling aliens and what they have
     to say without all the bullshit
     Spielberg flashlights shining into the
     camera and fear and all that crap.
     That this is true is its strength.

                    TONI
     Exactly. I knew you'd get it.

Mason smiles. Toni clutches the paperback.

                    TONI
                 (continuing)
     I've stayed away from the nightmare
     of trying to get a movie made in
     Hollywood, but this material is
     compelling me to do it. I think it's
     that important.

                    MASON
     It's going to be a bear to come up
     with a movie out of all this.

                    TONI
     These are evolved beings and I think
     it's vital to bring their message—
     the Divine Plan—to the world.

                    MASON
     A little of the Galaxians is going
     to go a long way. The question is
     how to present the material.

        THE GALAXIANS—THREE DRAFTS   III

                    TONI
        We'll ask them.

Mason doesn't understand.

                    TONI
                (continuing)
        We'll go to down to Atlanta and Kim
        will channel the Galaxians for us.
        They'll help us with the script.

Mason smiles unsurely.

                    TONI
                (continuing)
        You know, I know . . .

She points to Kim's photograph on the back of the book.

                    TONI
                (continuing)
        . . . Kim.

                    MASON
        Yeah?

                    TONI
        I read one of her books, called her,
        and she did a reading for me. It's
        not something she does for
        everyone. . . . I think she's very,
        very gifted.

                    MASON
        What do you mean "reading"?

                    TONI
        Kim channels Ascended Masters from
        higher dimensions. She asked them
        about me . . . they said . . .
                    (humbly)
        . . . I was destined to do great
        things on this planet, bring people
        together, create a new
        consciousness. They said it would be
        the third lifetime where I've been
        one of the leaders of society.

Mason looks at her . . . for a long unsure beat . . .
then the Waitress arrives, pad in hand.

Toni picks up her menu.

                    TONI
            (continuing; to Mason)
        You go.

                    MASON
        I'll have an uni/avocado handroll,
        yellowtail sushi, mira gai sashimi.
                    (to Toni)
        What do you want?

Toni looks up from the menu.

                    TONI
        I'll have a miso soup and salmon
        skin salad.

                    MASON
                (to the Waitress)
        Thank you.
                    (to Toni)
        What does Kim do?

                    TONI
        Since writing the book, Kim's been
        guided to lead spiritual guests. I
        just got back from Nassau with her.

Mason's surprised.

                    TONI
                (continuing)
        A group of us went there to
        reconfigure the magnetic vortexes and
        power points on the earth's
        electromagnetic grid connected to
        Atlantis. It's very profound work.

Mason studies Toni unsurely again, then . . .

                    MASON
        As for our deal: We'll be fifty/fifty
        partners, you pay for the option,
        you Executive Produce . . . I'll
        write and be guaranteed to direct.

Toni smiles.

                    TONI
        "Guaranteed"?

                    MASON
        Yup . . . otherwise you pay me to
        write the script.

                    TONI
                (after a beat)
        Okay, but I'd like to be Producer as
        well as Executive Producer because I
        want to be involved in all of the
        creative decisions.

                    MASON
        Executive Producer is a more
        important job.

                    TONI
        Can't I be both?

                    MASON
        Executive Producer and
        Producer . . .
                (after a long beat)
        . . . it's our deal . . . why not?

EXT. SKY - DAY

Cumulus clouds. A brilliant blue sky. A plane flies
through.

INT. AIRPLANE - DAY

Looking out the window, Mason turns to Toni, who's
sitting next to him.

                    MASON
        I hate flying.

                    TONI
        I think it's terrific you believe all
        this.

After a beat . . .

>   MASON
>   I don't.

>   TONI
>   Then, why . . . ?

>   MASON
>   I think it's really a commercial
>   project . . .
>   (with a hint of desperation)
>   . . . and I just gotta get out of
>   porn.

EXT. ATLANTA AIRPORT - DAY

A white stretch limousine parked at the curb. Mason
and Toni exit the terminal, climb into the limo, and
are swept away.

EXT. GEORGIA HOUSING TRACT - LATER THAT DAY

Million-dollar homes in a gated community. The
limousine pulls away from a large white modern
house. Mason videos the house as Toni rings the
bell. After a few moments, the front door opens.
Kim, forties, well coiffed in a Bette Midler sort of
way, smiles.

>   KIM
>   Welcome.

She kisses Toni.

>   TONI
>   This is Mason . . . Kim.

Mason and Kim shake hands.

                    MASON
          It's a real pleasure.

                    KIM
          Please come in. . . . How was your
          flight? Can I get you all some
          coffee?

INT. GEORGIA HOUSE - KITCHEN - DAY

Pastels, open and clean, a two-story vaulted ceiling,
filled with New Age art, mandalas, crucifixes, prayer
wheels, and religious gimcracks.

Kim brings a plate of fruit over to the glass kitchen
table as Mason adjusts his video camera on its tripod.
He shoots for a moment, then plays it back. He's
ready.

Kim sits.

                    MASON
          Okay, thanks for letting us come in
          here and talking with us . . . and
          letting us tape.

                    KIM
          When Toni called me . . . I had a
          feeling this was going to be
          something very special.
                    (smiling)
          I have a lot of ideas for the movie.

Toni grins.

                         TONI
          Me, too.

Mason smiles.

                         MASON
          Me, too.

Everyone's upbeat. A great beginning.

                         MASON
                      (continuing)
          Why don't we start . . . ?

He presses RECORD and frames his shot of Kim, who's a
little uncomfortable in front of the camera.

                    MASON'S VOICE
          This is Dr. Kim Daniels, author of,
          THE GALAXIANS, in her home in
          Georgia. This is the first interview.
                      (after a beat)
          Kim, if you would, tell us how you
          first made contact with the
          Galaxians.

                         KIM
          Well, they actually made contact
          with me. I was waiting for my
          clients at the Technical/Vocational
          Center at the University of Georgia
          where I was a career counselor for
          the faculty. I have a doctorate and
          a Department of Defense security
          clearance.

                    MASON'S VOICE
          A doctorate in?

Kim smiles proudly.

                         KIM
          Education.

                    MASON'S VOICE
          OK, you were telling us about your
          first contact with the
          Galaxians. . . .

                    KIM
          I was looking over
          assignments. . . .

INT. UNIVERSITY COUNSELING ROOM - SURVEILLANCE TAPE -
DAY

Sitting in the large empty conference room, Kim
checks her watch—apparently her appointments are
late—then sits at the conference table, pulls papers
out of the book bag and spreads out her work, a couple
of files, a fresh yellow pad, a cheap ballpoint pen.

                    KIM'S VOICE
          I was early and the room was empty.

She opens a file to a stack of sample résumés and
begins reading.

The yellow pad is still blank.

The pen lies beside it.

Kim reading intently.

                    KIM'S VOICE
                    (continuing)
          I was reading the first résumé when I
          heard a voice. . . .

Kim reading . . .

                    GENDERLESS VOICE
               Pick up a pen.

Kim looks up and turns to see who spoke.

No one there.

Kim turns the other way.

No one there either.

Weird.

INT. GEORGIA HOUSE - KITCHEN - DAY - CONT'D.

Mason leans forward. . . .

                    MASON
          What did the voice sound like?

                    KIM
          Hard to say . . . maybe like a
          man's voice, almost genderless,
          really . . . so I looked
          around . . . there was no one else
          in the room. I thought I must've
          been mistaken or something.

                    MASON
          What'd you do?

                              KIM
            Nothing. I went back to reading and
            after a few seconds I heard the
            voice again. . . .

INT. UNIVERSITY COUNSELING ROOM - DAY - CONT'D.

Kim reading the papers.

Another few beats . . .

                     GENDERLESS VOICE
                   (a bit more assertive)
                Pick up a pen.

Again, Kim looks around.

Still no one.

Kim looks down at the pen . . .

. . . next to the pad . . .

. . . and, after a moment, she picks it up.

Hefts it . . .

. . . then moves it over the pad . . .

. . . and touches the tip to the paper . . .

. . . and waits.

Okay, now what?

                    KIM'S VOICE
          So I did, I had a yellow pad
          there . . . and I just put the pen
          on the pad and waited.

The tip of the pen resting on the yellow of the
paper.

Waiting.

Kim looks around.

INT. GEORGIA HOUSE - KITCHEN - DAY - CONT'D.

Mason's into it.

                      MASON
          What was going through your mind?

                       KIM
          I didn't know. I thought it was odd,
          for sure . . . and I felt a little
          foolish doing it . . . so I just
          waited. . . .

INT. UNIVERSITY COUNSELING ROOM - DAY - CONT'D.

Kim shrugs.

                       KIM
                   (continuing)
          . . . and suddenly . . . my hand
          started to move.

Still waiting . . . then:

The tip of the pen quivers!

Kim can't believe it.

Her hand <u>is moved</u> awkwardly across the pad.

Ink being laid onto paper.

The pen moving across the paper.

                    KIM'S VOICE
          I wasn't controlling my hand . . .
          something else was.

Kim's clearly not in control of her hand. The pen
moves very slowly along the paper.

Arcing . . .

Purposeful.

An incredulous Kim watches.

The pen lifts up . . .

. . . starts again.

Kim watches . . . fascinated.

As her hand slowly, awkwardly continues writing.

Her hand starts a third time. . . .

Slowly . . . but constant.

Kim's hand arcs on the paper, then stops.

She waits.

Nothing.

It's over. She can feel it.

Kim takes a deep breath.

She lifts up the pen, and lays it down next to the pad. She studies the marks on the pad.

There are four of them. Crude shaky doodles.

Kim is totally baffled.

INT. GEORGIA HOUSE - KITCHEN - DAY - CONT'D.

Mason checks the fold-out screen on the camera. It's fine.

> MASON
> Were you scared?

> KIM
> No . . . I was, I guess, fascinated.
> I couldn't figure out what was going
> on.

> MASON
> What happened then?

> KIM
> Nothing. Afterwards, I went home,
> told Robert, my husband, about it.
> He was an Engineer at the time, a
> real smart guy, and he told me what
> I was doing was called "automatic
> writing." I'd never heard of it. I
> (more)

                    KIM (cont'd)
          tried it a couple of times after
          that . . . and I got much better at
          it very quickly . . . the pen
          started writing words. . . .

INT. GEORGIA HOUSE - NIGHT

A small house. Kim automatic writing on the yellow
pad in a small brightly lit room.

                    KIM'S VOICE
               (LAUGHING at the memory)
          The first words were "good day."
          It was extraordinary.

She writes GOOD DAY on the pad.

Kim stands up from the table . . .

. . . looks down at what she's written . . .

. . . and her hand covers her mouth in astonishment.

INT. GEORGIA HOUSE - KITCHEN - DAY

Kim continues.

                    KIM
          I practiced for about a week . . .
          getting faster and faster, then one
          night at home, Robert was watching
          TV, I was in the dining room. . . .

INT. GEORGIA HOUSE - DINING ROOM - NIGHT

Kim at the dining room table with her pen and
pad . . . practicing automatic writing.

She's writing faster than ever . . .

. . . quickly,

surely . . .

legibly.

INSERT ON PAPER

As Kim writes <u>We, the Galaxians, thank you for having
an open mind.</u>

Kim can't believe it.

Writing. Clear and legible.

She reads it and mouths the words.

Fascinating.

INT. GEORGIA HOUSE - KITCHEN - DAY - CONT'D

TIGHT SHOT through Mason's camera.

                    MASON'S VOICE
          You didn't think you were
          hallucinating?

                         KIM
          Not at all.

                    MASON'S VOICE
          You weren't worried you were going
          crazy?

Kim chuckles.

                    KIM
          Not at all. I thought something very
          important was happening. I wasn't
          sure what it was . . . but I took it
          as some kind of sign.

                 MASON'S VOICE
          And Robert?

Kim shrugs.

                    KIM
          Nothing.

                 MASON'S VOICE
          "Nothing"?

Kim nods.

                    KIM
          He was fine with it. Totally
          supportive.

EXT. GEORGIA HOUSE - BACKYARD - LATER THAT DAY

As Mason stretches by the kidney-shaped pool,
Toni freshens her makeup.

                    TONI
          I've heard a lot of channels.
          Kim's very clear . . . very
          precise.

                   MASON
          Pretty outrageous.

Kim waves from the house.

                              MASON
                          (continuing)
            Here we go.

And they head inside.

INT. GEORGIA HOUSE - OFFICE - MOMENTS LATER - DAY

Computers, books—spiritual, self-help, corporate and
computers—religious statuary, New Age slogans, framed
certificates on the walls.

Kim gets herself comfortable in her chair while Mason
sets up his video camera.

                              KIM
            I'm going to channel the Galaxians.
            Actually, I've felt them here with
            us this morning.

Kim smiles, then adjusts crystals around her.

Mason finishes fussing with his camera.

                              MASON
            I'm ready.

Kim, Toni, and Mason sit facing each other.
Everyone's excited.

Kim fine-tunes two crystals on the table next to her,
takes a deep breath, and closes her eyes.

                              KIM
            Okay . . . we should focus on the
            light . . . the clear light . . .

Toni closes her eyes.

                        KIM
                   (continuing)
          . . . clear out our minds . . .
          think of the purity. . . .

Kim quiets . . . concentrates.

Toni's eyes remain closed.

Mason studies the details . . . the tiny chrome studs
on Kim's Western shirt . . .

. . . the Nike running shoes . . .

. . . her beauty parlor hair . . .

. . . the country music makeup.

THE REST OF THE STORY

We didn't show Kim this draft. She had promised us some more channeling—specific answers to many specific questions, finally pinning the aliens down to much-needed and more much-asked-for visual descriptions—and didn't deliver after many promises. The script was evolving and we were moving on.

The producer, with one last polish, agrees to go with the draft. (A polish, by the way, is a rewrite that's really less than a regular rewrite, just the few final fixes before you send it out. The truth is, you can rewrite for ever. There isn't some finite "this is the right way the writing should be." The polish is those few, final rewrites—cleanups, if you will, to make the script finished.)

The producer had two A-list producers she was going to show the script to. I was excited. Finally, after over two years of writing, on our way.

The first producer she showed the script to gave it to his reader, as is normal. The reader didn't like it and they passed.

My producer immediately lost faith in the script and didn't want to show it anymore. She wanted a massive rewrite. When I asked her for her rewrite notes, she didn't have any. All she knew was what we had wasn't right.

I felt her lack of experience being rejected drove her decision. *Stigmata* took eight years to make. Many people passed. It only takes one to say yes, and you have to be persistent. But she couldn't hear me. She was freaked out by the rejection.

I was off on another project for three months and returned to *The Galaxians* after a call from the producer. She was now convinced the faux documentary approach was all wrong and produced new pages of Galaxian channeling and a transcript of a "brainstorming" session between her and Kim.

Their suggestions were:

Show positive examples of life in the Sixth Dimension

No negativity

Only light and good vibrations

Work is joyful

People living in harmony

People are respected

Abundance for all

The movie will reinvent the world with new thoughts

The film should show that the success of the Galaxian civilization is due to the fact they have mastered oneness

Huh?

What's the movie? Who are the characters? What's the rewrite?

Now we were going back, before square one, we were going back to conception.

Headline: "SCREENWRITER RUNS FOR HIS LIFE!"

The producer explained that the Galaxians said all the work (read: my writing) that's been done so far has been just "practice." Now the writing begins.

I was beginning to not like the Galaxians.

I agreed to read all the material and did, then called the producer. Before I could tell her I didn't feel their pages were a movie and that I was dropping out of the project, she said she now felt we didn't have a movie without the Galaxians appearing—for real—in the film. She told me she had asked them to agree to be filmed, but found them a little hard to pin down.

I totally supported this. It meant I didn't have to do any more writing and the ball was in Kim and the Galaxians' court. It was Kim's job to get the Galaxians to appear on film. If we could get that, I told her we could make a deal anywhere in town.

I'm still waiting for the date to schedule the shoot.

After a few more unproductive channeling sessions for which the producer had to pay Kim on an hourly basis, I told the producer in my gentlest manner that this was a farce, that these note sessions were a joke and I didn't believe it for a second. The producer was stunned.

Not listening to my warning, the producer had yet another meeting with Kim and the Galaxians. She asked me to read the notes because they were "very intriguing."

I read the notes. Same old, same old. They said we should come up with the story and they'll plug the fascinating new information into it.

After seven separate drafts and countless rewrites, I dropped out of the project.

Twelve

MY REWRITING HALL OF FAME

THE MOW PRODUCER

I WAS WRITING A MOVIE OF THE WEEK FOR TWO PRODUCING partners, working with the junior partner and enjoying a creative, productive relationship. Then came the notes meeting. The senior partner, an industry veteran—pipe, Gucci loafers, a house like an English manor in Hancock Park—came to the meeting a few minutes late, after his partner and I had gotten off to a great start, and he brought up the matter of how I used "continueds" in the script. Talk about a meeting stopper.

It seems he didn't agree with the way I used "continueds" when a character speaks in consecutive dialogue blocks. He very carefully, and I mean *very carefully*—in fact, I'd go as far to say very pedantically— went on to explain how and when "continueds" should and shouldn't be used.

At first, I explained the way I was using "continueds" was pre-ordained in the software I was using, but that fell on deaf ears as he strived lengthily to make his point. Sensing I was about to decompensate and tear the lips off his face before he knew what happened, I stopped defending and started agreeing and told him I would fix it in the next draft. His work done, the executive took a last pull off his pipe, excused himself, and exited. His partner spent the rest of our meeting apologizing profusely.

THE NETWORK EXECUTIVE

This is the executive to whom I originally used the phrase "The Writer is in the room" as a plea for him to stop bad-mouthing the writing, *my* writing. We were working on a series and had worked together before. We're friendly, we joke around, we have a good time with each other. That familiarity apparently made him feel he could, in a notes meeting, describe my writing as "cheesy" and "lame" and how the dialogue made him "want to vomit." Maybe familiarity breeds contempt.

Since then, he has, in later notes meetings, referred to one of my scripts as "an empty vessel," and a few scenes as "less than zero."

Headline: "SCREENWRITER HELD IN STRANGLING DEATH OF NETWORK EXECUTIVE"

THE BIG PRODUCTION COMPANY

I took over as supervising producer—responsible for the writing staff and turning out all the scripts—on a syndicated series a few years ago. It was the show's second year and the studio wanted changes. They didn't like the stories or the writing of the first season.

At a lunch in the studio's exclusive six-seater private lunch room was the head of the production company and his partner on the series, the head of another company, and me. The waiter served us. We ate. They talked. I perspired. They hired me. I was surprised.

NOTE: I'm a little embarrassed to admit that, as a rule, I try not to eat in front of people who are thinking of hiring me. Too many accident opportunities: debris between teeth, greasy drip stains on shirts, and—possibly the worst—the potential of spitting a glob of food onto the face of the person you're trying to impress. In situations like this I eat lightly and very carefully.

I hired a staff of two, developed stories, heard pitches, interviewed and hired freelancers, and we were off and running. About four weeks later, after having heard a ton of pitches and putting six stories into the works, the executive producer, out of the blue, says they're not happy with the writing of the first few stories. My writing.

Okay, I say, what can we do to fix them?

They said they'd like me to write more like the producer/writer from last year, the guy they fired, the writing they wanted so desperately to change.

I told them I would endeavor to write like the writer they didn't like, however I was cursed with the fact that I write like Tom Lazarus, and always will.

I think they were trying to get me to quit.

I didn't.

From there it was all downhill.

Less than five minutes later I was in my car.

Fired.

I made a settlement on my contract.

I had failed, but I walked away with enough money to have the time to sit down and write a screenplay, and I wrote *Stigmata*.

THE INDEPENDENT PRODUCER

Mr. Nothing Short of Brilliant. He had the money "in the bank" for production. "Nothing short of brilliant" was his note on the first draft of the screenplay he had asked me to write. I loved him, agreed with him that the script was brilliant, and we got along famously because he had the money "in the bank."

Three months later, after I learned the producer lied to me about almost everything including having the money "in the bank," he found a financier in San Francisco, who actually did have the money. Behind my back they had the script rewritten by the financier's son, a "film school graduate." After that betrayal, I took my script and went home and never spoke to the producer again.

I rewrote the script three more times, once with another producer, who referred to the development process with me as "the worst experience of his life." Ultimately it got made, in its original form, with yet another producer.

THE DEVELOPMENT EXECUTIVE

Here was a guy who was clearly in over his head. A company had an idea for a script and they hired me to write it. It was about stolen home videotapes (think Pamela Anderson and Tommy Lee). The company turned the script development over to their development executive, a man who I had suggested to the company for the post and they hired.

I turned in the first draft and I got notes. They were way off point . . . and really major.

Change the bad guy.

Change the motive.

Change the genre.

I resisted.

We argued.

He had suggestions that made our hero unsympathetic and unlikable. I, as carefully as I could—after all this was my friend—suggested that his changes would totally alter the script, change it from a mystery into a thriller, destroy what his bosses commissioned and what I had written. He didn't see it that way at all and the meeting ended with him saying "Don't think about the changes, just do what I say."

I did.

The rewrite was an embarrassment.

They brought in another writer after me, to do more of their changes and they made the film. The development executive was fired. He's still a friend. And he's still out of work.

Thirteen

THE BUSINESS OF REWRITES

IN THIS DAY AND AGE, BECAUSE, AMONG OTHER THINGS, PEOPLE at the studios and networks are in such a corporate/insecure/competitive/high stakes world, they cover their asses by hiring writer after writer on a project to make sure, in their boss's eyes, that they have done everything possible to make this project a success (see Chapter 1). This means typically more than one writer has written a finished script, and credits—the contributions each writer has made—have to be decided. The Writer's Guild of America, which arbitrates writing credits, takes care of that with an anonymous panel of three experienced writers who look at all the anonymously submitted writing and decide. There are strict rules and formulas carefully analyzing each writer's contributions and how that impacts on the credits. (If I told you what those rules and formulas are, I'd have to kill you.) Monies from residuals and production bonuses are dependent on the final credits.

For example, and I quote from the Writer's Guild Residuals Survivor Manual: "Residuals for theatrical and television motion pictures, including episodic programs, are allocated as follows: 'Written by'—100%; 'Screenplay/Teleplay by' (if a 'Story by' or 'Screen/Television Story by' credit is accorded)—75%; 'Story by' or 'Screen/Television Story by'—25%. In general, if no form of 'Story by' is accorded, 100% goes to the writer(s) receiving

'Screenplay or Teleplay by' credit. The residual for minor credits such as 'Adaptation by' is 10%. In that instance, the residual is allocated as follows: 'Adaptation by'—10%; 'Screenplay/Teleplay by'—65%; 'Story by'—25%."

Why is this important? Because it is not uncommon to sell a script in the six figures and have the residuals be more than the initial buy. It's all about money, and lots of it.

Because on *Stigmata,* my big moneymaking film with an impressive after-theatrical life, I had sole story and shared screenplay—first position, rather than story and sole screenplay credit; my payoff was diminished by thousands of dollars.

At the time of credit arbitration, I argued in my statement to the anonymous arbitrators that Writer B had not written enough to deserve credit. I, as Writer A, wrote a four-page history of the project, described the many, many drafts I did, gave a detailed analysis of what I wrote in the script and what Writer B had written. I told them that all of this added up to my deserving sole screenplay credit. I read Writer B's statement and it was a passionate argument why he felt he deserved to share credit.

I lost.

I thought the decision could have gone either way. At the time I was pissed at Writer B. With the luxury of time, I now believe the credit arbitration was fair. The bottom line is that Writer B contributed to getting the film made.

I've served on many credit arbitration panels for the Writer's Guild and I think it's a fair process. I'm very diligent and look at it like a mystery investigation. Finding the truth of each writer's contribution. Figuring it out. Getting beyond the writer's statement to the work itself and being fair and objective. It's fun. I've had more than a dozen credits arbitrated by the WGA and, in almost every case, even though I wasn't necessarily pleased, I thought the outcome was fair.

REWRITES FROM HELL

Knowing the dollars it means, rewriting sometimes brings out bad writing by bad writers. They get greedy and do things like changing all the names of the characters, rewriting scenes that don't need to be rewritten, changing things for the sake of changing them so they can own more of the script and receive more credit and get more money.

Fourteen

CHRONOLOGY OF A REWRITE

K'ANG MI

Now it's time to take it to another level.

Following are three drafts of the same script, *K'ang Mi,* an original screenplay I wrote about the abominable snowman. By reading these examples, one after another—in detail—you can see the chronology of a rewrite. It's a word-for-word, step-by-step, behind-the-scenes look at drafts of an actual rewrite. Included in the drafts are my explanations of why a particular rewrite was made, why I rewrote what I rewrote. The notes will—in the tinted boxes inserted into the scripts—follow each instance of rewriting.

For the first draft, the notes in the boxes explain why I wrote what I wrote. The rationale, if you will, for what is on the page.

By seeing actual examples of rewriting, you'll understand the potential for rewriting your own screenplays.

K'ANG MI
FIRST DRAFT

Written by Tom Lazarus

FADE IN:

INT. UNIVERSITY DIGITAL LAB - NIGHT - MAIN TITLES

Two silhouetted figures, a man and a woman, in front
of a huge digital monitor showing the earth from a
photography satellite.

>   MAN'S VOICE
>   This is from Comsat 104.

>   WOMAN'S VOICE
>   That's the one.

ON DIGITAL MONITOR

A hemispheric slice closer.

>   WOMAN'S VOICE
>   (continuing)
>   We're looking for longitude 92.2
>   degrees north by latitude 27.3
>   degrees south.

ON DIGITAL MONITOR

The north Indian/Chinese/Russian landmass with a
storm twisting out of the Indian Ocean.

ON THE MAN

He's ALLAN, scruffy beard, in need of a haircut, very
focused and proud of his nerdiness.

> ALLAN
> What kind of magnification are you
> looking for?

ON THE WOMAN

She's DR. LACY KENDRICKS, thirties, as beautiful as she is brilliant, much more intense than Allan, in a turtleneck with a flannel shirt over it, jeans, hiking boots.

> LACY
> To the wall. Go for it!

Allan smiles and types instructions into the computer.

ON DIGITAL MONITOR

ZOOMING in on northern India.

ON DIGITAL MONITOR

Individual characteristics become visible. Mountains, plains, snaking rivers reflecting the ruthless sun.

> Technical hocus-pocus is good.

ON DIGITAL MONITOR

TIGHTER on Tibet, 'then Bhutan, the heart of the Himalayas.

> Exotic locations are good. Taking reader/viewers to places that are far from their couches.

ON LACY

Smiling.

ON DIGITAL MONITOR

CLOSER ON the craggy, snow-covered mountains of Bhutan.

ON DIGITAL MONITOR

STILL CLOSER on Chomo Lhari, a vast and dangerous mountain.

                    LACY'S VOICE
          Incredible!

> Enthusiastic. Excited. Passionate about her beliefs. Our hero.

ON ALLAN

Smiling at Lacy's excitement.

And validation for it.

ON DIGITAL MONITOR

FOCUSED ON individual peaks, ice falls. The
photographic grain is now blown out, forming abstract
patterns.

You remember *Blow-Up*, don't you?

ON LACY

Studying the monitor intensely.

ON DIGITAL MONITOR

The image searches . . .

                    ALLAN'S VOICE
          I don't see anything.

                    LACY
          You have a spectroscopic filter?

She uses a thirteen-letter word. Reinforces her brilliance.

Allan types in commands.

ON DIGITAL MONITOR

The image changes. It's a series of grainy,
multicolor splotches.

ON LACY

Leaping out of her seat.

                    LACY
          There!

Allan doesn't see it. Lacy points to a spot on the
monitor.

                    LACY
                 (continuing)
          There!

Her finger points to a single greenish spot, just one
grain in a pointillist field of fuzzy dots.

                    LACY
                 (continuing)
          That's it!

He turns to her, then, finally . . .

                    ALLAN'S VOICE
          It is something.

Our hero is in the hunt.

EXT. NASA - HOUSTON - DAY

Behind the chain link, the sprawling, state-of-the-
art NASA Imaging Center bakes in the bright sun.

                    LACY'S VOICE
          I appreciate your taking the time to
          see me.

Right to it. No stage waits. No traveling shots. No airplane stock shot. No bullshit.
Telling the story fast.

INT. NASA IMAGING CENTER - DAY

A Senior TECHNICIAN, barely out of his teens, plugs a
CD into his computer. The grainy image of the tiny
green splotch on his monitor. Lacy points.

                         LACY
          There.

The Senior Technician works at the computer for a few
moments. and blows the image up even more.

Going to a higher authority. More sophisticated technology.

Lacy's eyes widen.

ON NASA MONITOR

The green dot fills the screen. There are no details,
just color, visual noise.

Lacy looks at the Senior Technician studying the
image, trying to enhance it.

                    SENIOR TECHNICIAN
          My guess is . . . it's an anomaly,
          some kind of photographic artifact.

Lacy shakes her head.

>   LACY
>   How can you be sure?

>   SENIOR TECHNICIAN
>   Does it appear on any other images
>   taken in the same area?

>   LACY
>   No.

>   SENIOR TECHNICIAN
>   What do you want me to say?

Lacy has no answer as the Senior Tech takes the CD
out of his machine.

>   SENIOR TECHNICIAN
>   (continuing)
>   What do you think it is?

But Lacy, CD in hand, is on her way to the door and
gone.

TITLES END

Hopefully, the hook is in and the reader/viewer wants to continue. Time for a major transition.

EXT. EMERSON COLLEGE - DAY

Stark modern additions to the old campus in the

golden autumn sunlight as leaves blow past the
students walking between classes.

Book bag in hand and scarf blowing behind her, Lacy
runs across the campus.

Running's better than walking. She is a woman of action.

>   LACY'S VOICE
>   Needless to say I was bummed out
>   about NASA's rather narrow view of
>   the data. . . .

"Bummed out." A teacher who uses slang. Everything counts.

INT. COLLEGE LECTURE HALL - DAY

A seminar class of thirty-five semi-interested
undergraduates sitting in the streamlined, sun-filled
room.

Not the old-fashioned movie lecture hall.

A hard copy of the fuzzy dots with the greenish one
in the center, projected on the video wall screen.
Pacing back and forth, Lacy lectures. . . .

>   LACY
>   (continuing)
>   . . . that they don't believe
>   there's a possibility that high in
>   this remote Himalayan mountain range
>   a valley, sheltered from the harsh
>   elements, could exist.

Impassioned, Lacy stops to make her point.

> LACY
> If such a valley exists, it could be
> the home, the sheltered environment
> to what the Bhutanese call K'ang Mi,
> the legendary man/beast of the
> Himalayas.

The students suddenly perk up.

Lacy smiles.

> LACY
> You heard me.

A student raises her hand. Lacy nods at her.

> STUDENT
> Are you talking about the abominable
> snowman?

Lacy sits on the table in front of the students.

                    LACY
          Good question. Let's talk about that
          for a second. There is ample
          evidence that the K'ang Mi, the
          yeti, the abominable snowman, it's
          been called many things, roam the
          wilderness areas of the world.

And now, the story is up and running, the hook is in, it's time for a little backstory.

The students are fascinated. At the back of the
class, an Asian student makes copious notes.

I do the "Asian student" for a reason. Another piece of information, with a promise
of more. There are no accidents.

                    LACY
          My theory is that the existence of
          such an upright hominid offers a new
          way to interpret heretofore
          ambiguous paleoanthropological
          evidence. I wouldn't be surprised,
          with the advent of sophisticated
          measuring technology, if hominid
          fossils once thought to be from the
          Middle Pleistocene or older periods
          may, in fact, be quite recent.

I'm laying the pipe to make the K'ang Mi believable. That's one of the big
challenges of this screenplay.

BELL.

Not a student jumps out of their seat.

A pleased Lacy smiles.

                    LACY
          We'll continue on Monday.

Lacy gathers her lecture notes as the class, BUZZING,
exits.

EXT. CHARLES RIVER - NIGHT

Through storm clouds, the full moon shines across the
water. A twelve-story apartment tower overlooking the
river. The wind blows cold off the water.

On the twelfth floor, a single light burns.

                    SHERPA'S VOICE
          It was third day out on Thyangboche
          that we saw the tracks.

INT. TWELFTH-FLOOR APARTMENT - NIGHT

Great view. Four hundred square feet of space. A bed,
a computer, books. The only light is from the
computer monitor where a SHERPA, never looking
directly into CAMERA, talking nervously.

                    SHERPA
          It was nineteen thousand feet. We
          followed the footprints . . .
                    (pausing)
          . . . prints bigger than any man's
          foot . . .

More. Right away. Keep the information coming. More setting the hook.

Sitting at her computer, sipping a mug of tea, Lacy
watches, makes notes on a yellow pad.

                    SHERPA
          Until up in the distance, fifteen
          meters away . . . there . . .

Lacy stops writing and studies the screen.

                    SHERPA
                    (continuing)
          It was . . .
                    (motioning with his hand)
          . . . three meters high, covered
          with hair . . . it was the . . .
                    (in awe)
          . . . the K'ang Mi.

The screen FREEZES.

Not theory anymore. The story progresses.

INT. LACY'S APARTMENT - KITCHEN - NIGHT

Lacy pours herself a mug of tea and walks to the
large window and looks out into the night.

```
LACY'S POV

Looking into Cambridge. The city is alive. The WIND
WHISTLES eerily against the building . . . almost an
animal's cry.
```

A continuing criticism of my writing is that I don't write big enough. When I do, like write "an animal's cry," it feels over-the-top to me.

```
INT. LACY'S APARTMENT - NIGHT

Lacy turns away from the window, moves to the bed,
and lies down. Her eyes continue to blink with
thought.

INT. EMERSON COLLEGE - ADMINISTRATION BUILDING - DAY

DEAN HAMPTON, mid-fifties, an energetic woman, meets
with the note-taking Asian student from Lacy's class.
```

The minor mystery of the Asian student pays off.

```
INT. LACY'S APARTMENT - DAY

Sun everywhere. On the wall behind the computer
monitor, folk drawings of man/beasts labeled FEIFEI
from China and BATUTUT from Borneo and KAKUNDARI and
KILOMBA from the Congo.
```

Research is a good thing. It helps sell your ideas. A little goes a long way.

```
On the computer screen, ERIC SHIPTON, an Australian
in his thirties, talks into CAMERA.
```

                    ERIC SHIPTON
        It was on the Menlung glacier at
        about eighteen thousand feet we first
        took the photographs of the prints
        in the snow.

Lots of information . . . all to lend credibility to Lacy's search.

In sweats and running shoes, Lacy sits at her
keyboard.

                    ERIC SHIPTON
        We did a computer projection, based
        on weight and displacement
        variables.

ON MONITOR

A computer-generated 3-D hologram of a large, biped
mammal, a cross between a man and a bear.

Delivering the K'ang Mi before I actually can story-wise. A constant flow of new
material.

                    PROJECTIONS

HEIGHT: 8' 2.5"

WEIGHT: 389 LBS.

STRENGTH TO AVERAGE HUMAN - 145.54%

SPEED FOR 100 METERS - 10.145 SECONDS.

Lacy is blown away, then . . .

                    LACY
          But, you didn't see . . . ?

Shipton shakes his head.

The PHONE RINGS.

                    LACY
             (continuing; to Shipton)
          Hold on, please . . .
                  (answering the phone)
          Hi, it's Lacy.

INT. DEAN HAMPTON'S OFFICE - DAY

A troubled Dean Hampton stands stiffly behind her desk
talking into a phone headset.

                 DEAN HAMPTON
          We have a little bit of a . . . of a
          situation.

EXT. EMERSON COLLEGE CAMPUS - DAY

In her serious teacher double-breasted suit, Lacy
walks with Dean Hampton under the canopy of fall-
colored trees.

                 DEAN HAMPTON
          I'm terribly disturbed by reports
          you're straying from your approved
          curriculum.

Let the obstacles begin. Page 11. A different state for our hero to exist in.

Lacy LAUGHS.

                    LACY
          Please. This time of year is
          notorious for students going crazy,
          you know that.

                    DEAN HAMPTON
          I'm glad you're amused. Lacy, you're
          teaching anthropology and
          paleontology, not science fiction.

They stop as they reach the large pigeon-stained
statue of the founder, Dunkirk Emerson, standing with
a walking stick in one hand and an open book in the
other.

                    LACY
          The Kodiak bear was discovered in
          1899. The mountain gorilla wasn't
          known until 1901.

I love research.

                    DEAN HAMPTON
          I'm not sure that's relevant.

                    LACY
          In 1975 a new species of shark was
          found. It is not outside of the
          realm of possibility, of
          possibility, that a K'ang Mi exists.
                    (passionate)
          It is that possibility that I'm
          teaching, that potential.

We like her for being smart and passionate about what she believes.

                    DEAN HAMPTON
          Well, stop.

Lacy turns away angrily, then just as quickly, turns
back, even more passionately. . . .

                         LACY
               Stop getting students interested?
               Stop getting them curious? Stop
               challenging them?

Dean Hampton studies her.

                    DEAN HAMPTON
               I have to tell you, this isn't the
               first complaint.

Lacy throws up her hands.

                         LACY
               I can't teach a curriculum I don't
               believe in.

After a beat . . .

                    DEAN HAMPTON
               I guess that says it all.

She holds out her hand to shake.

```
                    DEAN HAMPTON
          I'll get a replacement for you for
          tomorrow's classes. I'm sorry it had
          to end this way.

Lacy's stunned.
```

The obstacle plays out. And everything was going so well.

```
Dean Hampton shakes her hand.

                    DEAN HAMPTON
                      (distant)
          I've enjoyed having you on the
          faculty. Good luck.

And she spins and walks away.

Hand still out, Lacy is absolutely speechless.
```

Our hero in trouble.

```
INT. LACY'S APARTMENT - NIGHT

No light on. With much the same expression she had
with Dean Hampton, Lacy sits at her kitchen table
with a mug of tea.

After a long, thoughtful moment, Lacy finally breaks
into a smile . . . which spreads into a joyous grin.
```

A decision has been made.

EXT. PUBLIC SCHOOL PARKING LOT - DAY

The double-breasted suit Lacy was wearing with Dean
Hampton is featured prominently on a rack in the
NEIGHBORHOOD TAG SALE of Lacy's stuff.

Pictures tell a story

Books, shoes, kitchen items, what looks like Lacy's
whole life, being picked over by neighbors and
bargain hunters in search for treasures.

WALTER, a man in jeans and a barn coat, talks with
Lacy, who's positively beaming.

> WALTER
> My guess is you have a wrongful
> termination lawsuit against the
> college.

A smiling Lacy shakes her head.

> LACY
> Way too negative. I've got better
> things to do with my time.

That's why they're called heroes, folks.

> WALTER
> You can't use the money?

Lacy takes a few bills for some kitchen items, then
turns back to Walter.

                    LACY
          That's what I'm doing out here,
          right?

Not sure about the last exchange. I hope I rewrote it in the next draft.

EXT. BOSTON HOSPITAL - DAY

One of the huge '60s monstrosities . . . a huge box,
slabs of concrete, small windows.

INT. BOSTON HOSPITAL - WARD - DAY

A faded black-and-white photograph of Mt. Everest
taped on the wall.

Lacy sits next to the hospital bed tape recording an
OLD TIBETAN, whose eyes are foggy white with
blindness.

                    OLD TIBETAN
          We found a yeti scalp in a monastery
          in Khumjun. That was . . .
                    (a long beat)
          . . . was with Sir Edmund on the
          1960 expedition to find the K'ang Mi.

                    LACY
          The museum discounted the find,
          saying the scalp was really the skin
          of a Himalayan antelope, the serow.

The Old Tibetan shrugs. He doesn't care.

Lacy smiles.

>   LACY
>   (continuing)
>   I examined their lab reports. The
>   mites found on that scalp were
>   actually very different than mites
>   found on serow pelts.

> More research. Keeps reinforcing the possibility/probability of all this.

The Old Tibetan slowly nods.

>   OLD TIBETAN
>   I have been to Thyangboche and
>   Pangboche, I have seen the
>   skins. . . .

The Old Tibetan puts his hand on Lacy's wrist.

>   OLD TIBETAN
>   (continuing)
>   As a boy, my father gave to the
>   museum in London . . .

The Old Tibetan opens his mouth wide . . . he has no
teeth . . . and points inside.

>   OLD TIBETAN
>   (continuing)
>   . . . K'ang Mi.

Lacy studies him.

Lacy tries to understand. The Old Tibetan points into
his mouth again, then . . .

                    OLD TIBETAN
                    (continuing)
          K'ang Mi.

EXT. NEW YORK CITY - HELICOPTER SHOT - DAY

Gliding over Central Park, over Central Park West to
the venerable Museum of Natural History with snaking
lines of school kids climbing the steps and hot dog
vendors hawking their greasy wares.

Lacy rushes down windswept Central Park West, then
hurries up the steps of the museum and enters.

INT. MUSEUM LIBRARY - OFFICE - DAY

A digital display runs numbers and dates ends on
AUGUST 12, 1937, 5:00 P.M.

A YOUNG ASIAN MAN in a gray cotton jacket looks up
from the computer.

                    YOUNG MAN
          We're digitized back to August 12,
          1937 . . . sorry.

INT. MUSEUM LIBRARY - STORAGE - LATER THAT DAY

Stuffed specimen in dusty bell jars.

Books upon books. Old paper files. It's the back rooms.

Log books with faded green canvas covers.

Feels like another century. The opposite of how we opened.

Notations made in beautifully written nineteenth-century ink curlicues.

Lacy uses a magnifying glass as she goes down the long lists of objects logged into the museum's collection.

Our proactive hero.

A YOUNG ASIAN MAN in a gray cotton staff jacket enters rockin' to his Walkman.

Not clear why this guy is Asian, too.

>   YOUNG MAN
>   Dr. Kendricks, how long are you
>   going to want to be in here today?

Lacy smiles. She's tired.

>   LACY
>   Right up to closing.

The Young Man nods.

                         YOUNG MAN
                     (sympathetically)
                  You want a soda, something?

Lacy holds up her thermos.

                           LACY
                  Just keep all knives and sharp
                  object away from me, okay?

                         YOUNG MAN
                  What year are you up to?

Lacy checks the cover of the book.

                           LACY
            1886.

                         YOUNG MAN
                       (lying badly)
                  Well, you're moving right along.

Lacy LAUGHS.

The Young Man smiles and walks out, his footsteps
ECHOING crisply on the shiny linoleum floors.

Lacy returns to the log book and goes down the list
of entries with the magnifying glass, which she puts
down, and with her eyes never leaving the log book,
unscrews the top of the thermos bottle and pours
herself the last of the hot tea.

As she's screwing on the top . . . she stops. Lacy puts
down the thermos and picks the magnifying glass back up.

THRU THE MAGNIFYING GLASS

to the nineteenth-century script:

One K'ang Mi incisor. 3.678 mm by 1.276 mm.

Thangboche Monastery. No. 45.612-AR.

LOANED TO NATURAL HISTORY MUSEUM OF LONDON, October 5, 1886.

In different handwriting . . .

NOT RETURNED AS OF January 23, 1909.

Lacy can't believe her eyes.

The track gets warmer. New stuff entering mix.

EXT. LONDON - DAY

The London Museum of Natural History.

> LACY'S VOICE
> Number 45.612-AR.

> CLERK'S VOICE
> (British accent)
> One moment.

INT. LONDON MUSEUM OF NATURAL HISTORY - RESEARCH - DAY

Lacy sits on the hard wooden bench, then stands and walks over to the research desk as a WELL-DRESSED CLERK returns holding a yellowed item card.

                    CLERK
          I'm a tad embarrassed to say we
          actually don't know where that item
          is. We actually have no record of it
          whatsoever. It's inexplicable,
          really.

A different dialogue style indicates a Brit.

                    LACY
          It's here . . . somewhere?

The Clerk looks the card over, then slowly nods.

                    CLERK
          That would be the indication . . .
          but as to precisely where . . .

The Clerk doesn't know what to say.

The hunt continues.

INT. LONDON PUB - NIGHT

Raucous drinkers. Lacy at the bar nursing an ale and
feeling happy.

                    MAN'S VOICE
          I'd buy you another one.

Lacy turns. It's EVAN, ruddy cheeked, in a tweed
jacket, a school tie, and a warm smile.

Lacy returns his smile.

> LACY
> I'd like that.

> EVAN
> You're from the States, then?

> LACY
> Last time I looked.

Evan LAUGHS.

> EVAN
> Well, I won't hold that against you.

Lacy LAUGHS.

> EVAN
> My name's Evan Wainwright.

> LACY
> Lacy Kendricks. What do you do
> besides hang out in pubs?

> EVAN
> I'm a bit of a writer.

                              LACY
             Well, I won't hold that against you.

They LAUGH together.

INT. SPECIMEN STORAGE, LONDON MUSEUM - DAY

Boxes, crates, of all sizes, with every kind of
label, stacked a dozen deep nearly to the ceiling.

Lacy examines a small, tooth-sized, meticulously
crafted little wood crate.

With a small electric screwdriver, she unscrews the
six screws on one side and excitedly lifts off the
crate side.

Inside is a <u>Lacracerian Toricolethum,</u> a horrifying-
looking specimen of horned beetle.

After her initial surprise, disappointment.

EXT. LONDON - NIGHT

With Evan by her side, Lacy walking down the crowded
shopping street.

                              EVAN
                It isn't healthy to be cooped up in
                that stuffy old museum all day long.
                You need to get your blood flowing.

                              LACY
                And how do you suggest I do that?

Evan stops and gives her a tentative kiss.

                    EVAN
        A bout of lovemaking would probably
        fit the bill.

Lacy LAUGHS.

                    EVAN
                 (continuing)
        Is it that far-fetched?

Lacy leans up, kisses Evan tenderly and smiles.

                    LACY
        Not that far-fetched.

                    EVAN
        Why not take time off, we'll go out
        into the country.

Lacy smiles back at him, then puts her hand on his.

                    LACY
        I have three more days . . . that's
        it, no more money.

                    EVAN
                 (gently)
        Do you need any help, then?

She touches his cheek.

                    LACY
        You're sweet.
                 (shaking her head)
        I'll toss all my money away on this,
        not yours.

```
INT. SPECIMEN STORAGE, LONDON MUSEUM - DAY

Another small crate. Lacy prying it open.

Inside, a nearly perfect quartz crystal. It glints in
the work lights. She's bummed.

She closes that box and picks up another. Lacy's
tired. There's no marking on the box of any kind.
Unable to squash her excitement, Lacy quickly forces
the box open.

Inside is a single small bone . . . nothing.

Disappointed, Lacy closes the box.

Lacy empties the last of the tea out of the thermos
and looks at the unopened stack of two dozen small
specimen cases.

She takes a deep tired breath, then grabs a small
screwdriver, pries open the crate, unpacks the straw
revealing . . .

. . . a stained incisor!
```

```
A glorious thing: shiny, worn, huge.

Lacy checks the faded scrawl and number on the item
card.
```

460612-AR

Pomangranuts illeriama

                  LACY
      But, that's not . . .

She doesn't finish . . . and breaks into a broad
smile.

INT. LONDON HOTEL ROOM - NIGHT

Evan and Lacy lying contently in bed after making
love.

                  LACY
      OK, you got my blood flowing, are you
      happy?

Not sure about that transition.

Evan laughs.

                  EVAN
      Delighted.
        (looking at her, then nodding)
      OK, now.

Lacy bolts up and turns on the lamp on the night table.

She pulls out the small packing box and opens it.

She carefully takes out the incisor and shows it to
Evan, who shrugs.

                    EVAN
                 (continuing)
        It's a bloody tooth.

                    LACY
        Exactly, but it's too large for a
        human . . .

Evan studies it.

                 LACY'S VOICE
                 (continued)
        . . . too developed for a gorilla.

                    EVAN
        What do you think it is?

                    LACY
        The needle in the haystack, the
        missing K'ang Mi incisor, the same
        number, it's it.

And she smiles with excitement.

                    LACY
                 (continuing)
        It's my hard evidence.

INT. DATING LAB - LONDON - DAY

A huge potassium/argon dater.

Two gray-smocked Technicians work on the controls.

Lacy watches with interest as the incisor is placed
on the titanium caddy.

It slides into the cage and the thick glass door slides down.

The Technician wing-nuts the compartment closed.

The red light turns green.

Lacy watches from behind the control board.

The digital display reads <u>1000 A.D.</u>

Lacy gasps, then pumps her arm happily.

The Technician walks over to the ecstatic Lacy.

> TECHNICIAN
> It's nearly contemporary.

> LACY
> I know. I saw!

Feels like too much science already.

EXT. ROADWAY - NIGHT

Evan's car exits the roundabout toward Heathrow. Lacy's with him.

> LACY'S VOICE
> I'm so glad you bought me that drink.

EXT. HEATHROW TERMINAL - NIGHT

Evan's car parks in the no-parking zone. Lacy puts her hand on his.

                    EVAN
          Is that all?

INT. EVAN'S CAR - NIGHT

Lacy kisses him.

                    LACY
          I need a favor.

Evan smiles as Lacy hands him the incisor case.

                    EVAN
          You need me to accept stolen
          merchandise?

Lacy nods.

                    LACY
          And drop it off back at the museum,
          say you found it.

                    EVAN
          And when they arrest me?

Lacy kisses him again.

                    LACY
          I'll be on a plane.

Evan LAUGHS.

                    EVAN
          You are one, I'll tell you that.

                    LACY
        Thanks for everything. It's been
        real fun.

                    EVAN
                  (emotional)
            Lace . . .

She puts her finger to his lips, stopping him.

                    LACY
                  (tenderly)
            Let's leave it at that. It's been
            real fun.

Evan smiles.

                    EVAN
                (affectionately)
            It's been real fun.

They embrace fondly, then Lacy climbs out, pulls on
her backpack, and runs into the terminal.

Evan watches her as she turns, waves, then disappears
inside.

He's going to miss her.

At least he's not just a love interest. He has some story function.

EXT. WASHINGTON, D.C. - DAY

The stodgy National Geographic Society's
headquarters.

INT. NATIONAL GEOGRAPHIC OFFICE - DAY

Ornate and filled with the exotic plunder of a
thousand expeditions.

Lacy sits in front of the ASSISTANT DIRECTOR'S
antique desk. He's midthirties, Ivy League, a bit
full of himself and looking to get her out of his
office.

>   ASSISTANT DIRECTOR
>   I'm sorry. Your project really comes
>   a little below our radar.

Another obstacle.

>   LACY
>   What does that mean?

The Assistant Director stands up.

>   ASSISTANT DIRECTOR
>   We're going to be funding more
>   mainstream projects this year.
>   (continuing)
>   But, if I'm right . . .

He holds out his hand and smiles.

>   ASSISTANT DIRECTOR
>   (continuing)
>   Well, then I'm sure you'll be back.

EXT. EXPLORERS CLUB - DAY

The beaux arts center for adventurers.

                COMMANDER GARRARD'S VOICE
           We're really not in the Bigfoot
           business. . . .

Another one.

INT. EXPLORERS CLUB - HALLWAY - DAY

A large, dusty buffalo head on the wall.

Lacy walks with COMMANDER GARRARD, a thin man with an
unfortunately drooping handlebar mustache and a game
left leg.

                COMMANDER GARRARD
           Good luck to you. Good hunting.

A disappointed Lacy shakes the Commander's hand and
exits unhappily.

EXT. NEW YORK CITY - DOWNTOWN LOFT - SUNSET

The sun reflects in the large industrial windows.

INT. MATTHEW HARDAWAY'S LOFT - DAY

MATTHEW HARDAWAY is a handsome man.

                HARDAWAY
           I'm very impressed.

Midthirties, expensively dressed in a Brooks Brothers
button-down shirt, pressed jeans, and hand-tooled
ostrich Tony Lamas, Hardaway hands Lacy a drink.

                    HARDAWAY
            That was Cutty straight up?

Lacy smiles and nods.

On the table in front of them, maps of the Himalayas,
large color slides of the incisor from all angles,
drawings of the man/beasts.

                    HARDAWAY
                    (continuing)
            How many days do you see the
            expedition taking?

Hardaway stands close to her.

                    LACY
                    (excited)
            Once we're in Bhutan, it'll take a
            day to get to the Chomo Lhari,
            then . . .
                    (smiling)
            . . . when the adventure
            begins . . . who knows.

Hardaway nods as he looks over Lacy's materials.

                    HARDAWAY
            This is really fascinating stuff.

He puts his hand on her shoulder.

                    HARDAWAY
                    (seductive)
        And you are equally as fascinating.

Lacy smiles, turns away, then walks over to the
window and the view uptown of Manhattan's lights
coming on.

Everyone approaches her sexually.

                     LACY
          So, is there a possibility you'd
          fund this?

Hardaway smiles at her.

                    HARDAWAY
          You're still here.

                     LACY
          How do we take the next step?

He smiles seductively.

                    HARDAWAY
          Well, that depends on the step we're
          talking about.

Looks like an adversary to me.

She smiles back.

                    LACY
          I put the cost of the expedition at
          a million dollars. I can show you
          the budget.

Hardaway is unfazed.

                    HARDAWAY
          And if you find something?

Lacy doesn't understand the question.

                    HARDAWAY
                    (continuing)
          Let's say the expedition finds this
          abominable snowman, who owns it?

Lacy studies him.

                    LACY
          No one owns anyone else.

His eyes blink with thought.

This isn't going to be easy.

Lacy moves closer to him, puts her hand on his arm,
looks right in his eyes.

Our hero plays Hardaway's game.

                    LACY
          I think it's going to be the first
          great adventure of the new century.

He studies her for a long moment, then nods.

> HARDAWAY
> I'll have contracts drawn up.

Lacy can't believe it.

She holds out her hand.

> LACY
> Deal?

> HARDAWAY
> Deal.

He gives her a hug . . . and holds it a little too long.

The game is still being played.

> HARDAWAY
> The publicity alone is worth more
> than a million.

Lacy laughs in happy disbelief as she gently pulls away from him. . . .

But Hardaway's not finished.

> HARDAWAY
> (continuing)
> It has to be called the Hardaway
> Expedition.

                    LACY
                (after a beat)
        OK.

                    HARDAWAY
        The find has to be called Hardaway
        Man.

    She looks at him for even a longer beat.

                    LACY
        I'm not sure. . . .

                    HARDAWAY
                (interrupting)
        And I go along on the expedition.

    Lacy looks at him in disbelief. . . .

This is going to be tougher than she thinks.

                                        CUT TO:

    EXT. THE HIMALAYAS - DAY

    The staggering snowy crest of the Himalayas tower
    over the tiny Buddhist kingdom of Bhutan. BUDDHIST
    TRANCE MUSIC plays.

Decision made. Twenty-eight pages in. Big transition.

    The notes in the previous draft were about the writing. What I
was trying to accomplish with the writing. Those pages were not
the first time through; they represent five drafts.

The notes in this next draft highlight the rewrites.

<u>**K'ANG MI**</u>
<u>**SECOND DRAFT**</u>

by Tom Lazarus

FADE IN:

BLACK SCREEN

Jumpy white titles in <u>Chinese.</u> The sound of WIND
BLOWING.

BLACK AND WHITE - WIND CONTINUES

Old film footage of the Himalayas, crudely cut
together, slightly speeded up, of the sunset glaring
off the snow.

BLACK AND WHITE - WIND CONTINUES

PANNING across the snow. In the distance, running
jerkily, three large figures, loping really, appearing
to be carrying large sticks.

The images are blurry and handheld, hard to make out,
as the light fades.

The figures, man/beasts, run faster . . . they're
chasing something . . .

. . . something smaller, running in fear.

A new opening.

BLACK AND WHITE - WIND CONTINUES

TELEPHOTO. Even less light. CLOSE UP of the figures
catching their prey. Blurry silhouettes, thrashing
around, fighting, violent, animalistic,
murderous . . .

Starting closer to the spine of the mystery sooner. Get to the abominable
snowman faster. That's what I have to sell.

                                              CUT TO:

BLACK SCREEN

The SOUNDS OF A COMPUTER PROCESSING . . .

FADE IN:

INT. UNIVERSITY DIGITAL LAB - NIGHT - MAIN TITLES

Two silhouetted figures, a man and a woman, in front
of a huge digital monitor showing the earth from a
photography satellite.

                    MAN'S VOICE
          This is Comsat 104.

ON DIGITAL MONITOR

A hemispheric slice closer.

                    WOMAN'S VOICE
                    (continuing)
          We're looking for longitude 92.2
          degrees north by latitude 27.3
          degrees south.

ON DIGITAL MONITOR

The north Indian/Chinese/Russian landmass with a
storm twisting out of the Indian Ocean.

ON THE MAN

He's ALLAN, gnarly sideburns, striped shirt and tie.

Very focused and unaware of his nerdiness.

> ALLAN
> What kind of magnification are you
> looking for?

ON THE WOMAN

She's DR. LACY KENDRICKS, thirties, as beautiful as
she is brilliant, much more intense than Allan, much
more alive and energized,

in a turtleneck with a flannel shirt over it, jeans,
hiking boots, into it big-time.

> LACY
> To the wall. Go for it!

Allan smiles and types instructions into the
computer.

ON DIGITAL MONITOR

ZOOMING in on northern India.

> Took out Digital Monitor slug line as redundant.

Individual characteristics become visible. Mountains, plains, snaking rivers reflecting the ruthless sun.

TIGHTER on Tibet, then Bhutan, the heart of the Himalayas.

Lacy smiles.

> A more concise way to write that. No slug line.

ON DIGITAL MONITOR

> Another slug line deletion to simplify.

CLOSER ON the craggy, snow-covered mountains of Bhutan.

STILL CLOSER ON the Chomo Lhari range, a vast and dangerous mountain. Lacy's blown away.

> Action instead of dialogue.

Allan smiles at Lacy's excitement.

> Deletion of slug line for simplification.

ON DIGITAL MONITOR

FOCUSED ON individual peaks, ice falls. The
photographic grain is now blown up, forming abstract
patterns.

Lacy studying the monitor intensely.

Deletion of slug line.

The image searches . . .

> LACY'S VOICE
> I don't see anything.

> ALLAN'S VOICE
> Let me try the spectroscopic filter.

Switched dialogue. More appropriate to the characters.

Allan types in commands.

Deletion of another slug line.

The image changes. It's a field

Changed from "series."

of grainy, multicolor splotches.

Yet another slug line deletion. Each time I do that I speed the read along. This
used to be the opening scene.

Lacy leaps out of her seat.

                    LACY
          There!

Deletion of Allan dialogue to give the scene more to Lacy.

Allan doesn't see it.

Lacy rushes

Adding action.

to the monitor and points to a spot on the screen.

                    LACY
          There!

Her finger points to a single green

Changed from "greenish," which I use later.

spot, just one grain in a pointillist field of fuzzy
dots.

                    LACY
          That's it!

He turns to her, then finally, almost reluctantly . . .

Added "reluctantly" to better communicate the attitude of the character.

```
                    ALLAN'S VOICE
          It is something.


Lacy lights up.

                         LACY
              Proof!


                         ALLAN
              It could be an artifact of the lens,
              in transmission . . .


Allan's not so sure.

TITLES END
```

Deletion of redundant NASA imaging center scene.

```
EXT. EMERSON COLLEGE - DAY

Stark modern additions to the old campus in the
golden autumn sunlight as leaves blow past the
students walking between classes.

Book bag in hand and scarf blowing behind her, Lacy
runs across the campus.

                    LACY'S VOICE
              My theory is that high in this
              remote Himalayan mountain
              range . . .
```

Revised dialogue to get to it sooner.

INT. COLLEGE LECTURE HALL - DAY

A seminar class of thirty-five semi-interested
undergraduates sitting in the streamlined, sun-filled
room. Pacing back and forth, Lacy lectures . . .

Deletion of wordy stage direction to get to main character sooner.

                    LACY
                (continuing)
           . . . there's a valley, sheltered
           from the harsh elements.

A hard copy of the fuzzy dots with the greenish

The reason I changed the earlier "greenish" to "green."

one in the center, projected on the video wall
screen.

                    LACY
                (passionate)
           This valley could be the home of
           what the Bhutanese call K'ang Mi,
           the legendary man/beast of the
           Himalayas.

Simplified dialogue.

An electric charge goes through the students.

Rewriting to sell the moment more.

Lacy smiles.

A student's hand thrusts into the air.

                    STUDENT
          Are you talking about the abominable
          snowman?

Lacy sits on the table.

                    LACY
          If the K'ang Mi does exist, it
          would offer a new way to interpret
          heretofore ambiguous
          paleoanthropological evidence.
          Hominid fossils once thought to be
          from the Middle Pleistocene or
          older periods may, in fact, be
          quite recent.

The students are fascinated. At the back of the
class, an Asian student makes copious notes.

                    LACY
                 (continuing)
          There is more than ample evidence
          that man/beasts, K'ang Mi,
          abominable snowman, Sasquatch, call
          them what you will, roam the
          wilderness areas of the world.

BELL.

Shorter, more pointed dialogue. A new reason—scientific research—for Lacy's
interest in the K'ang Mi. One of the foundations of the story.

Not a student jumps out of their seat.

A pleased Lacy smiles.

> LACY
>
> We'll continue on Monday.

GROAN. Lacy gathers her lecture notes as the class,
BUZZING, exits. The note-taking Asian student is
among the last to leave.

> Better setting up this moment. Something's about to happen.

EXT. CHARLES RIVER - NIGHT

Through storm clouds, the full moon shines across the
water.

A twelve-story apartment tower overlooking the river.
The wind blows cold off the water . . . sounding
almost like an ANIMAL'S CRY.

> More evocative stage direction.

On the twelfth floor, a single light burns.

> ERIC SHIPTON'S VOICE
>
> I have just a second before my
> flight.

> Deletion of Sherpa scene and the introduction of Dean Hampton to make story
> happen faster.

INT. TWELFTH-FLOOR APARTMENT - NIGHT

Great view. Seven hundred square feet of space. A
bed, a computer, books.

> LACY'S VOICE
> What altitude?

On the wall behind the computer monitor, folk drawings
of man/beasts labeled FEIFEI from China and BATUTUT
from Borneo and KAKUNDARI and KILOMBA from the Congo.

> ERIC SHIPTON'S VOICE
> It was at about eighteen thousand
> feet, on the Menlung glacier. There
> were two sets of footprints in the
> snow.

In sweats and running shoes, Lacy sits at her
keyboard, fascinated and taking notes.

> LACY
> I've seen the photographs. Very
> persuasive.

On the computer screen, ERIC SHIPTON, an Australian
in his thirties, talks into CAMERA. He types on his
computer.

> ERIC SHIPTON
> We did a computer extrapolation,
> based on weight and displacement
> variables.

ON MONITOR

A rotating computer-generated 3-D hologram of a

large, biped mammal, a cross between a man and a
bear.

K'ANG MI PROJECTIONS

HEIGHT: 8' 2.5"

WEIGHT: 389 LBS.

STRENGTH TO AVERAGE HUMAN - 165.54%

SPEED FOR 100 METERS - 10.145 SECONDS.

Lacy is blown away, then . . .

                    LACY
        But, you didn't see? . . .

Shipton shakes his head.

The PHONE RINGS.

                    LACY
              (continuing; to Shipton)
        Hold on, please. . . .
                  (answering the phone)
        Hi, it's Lacy.

INT. DEAN HAMPTON'S OFFICE - NIGHT

A troubled Dean Hampton behind her desk talking on
the phone.

Revised stage direction.

                    DEAN HAMPTON
          It's Dean Hampton. We have a little
          bit of a . . . of a situation.

The Asian Student watches the Dean on the phone.

At night? What?!

EXT. EMERSON COLLEGE CAMPUS - THE NEXT MORNING

In her serious college-instructor double-breasted
suit, Lacy walks with Dean Hampton, exits the
Administration Building, and walks down the tree-
lined pathway.

Expanded stage direction. Deletion of dialogue to get right to it.

                    DEAN HAMPTON
          Lacy, you're teaching anthropology
          and paleontology, not science
          fiction.

They stop as they reach the large pigeon-stained
statue of the founder, Dunkirk Emerson, standing with
a walking stick in one hand and an open book in the
other.

                    LACY
          The Kodiak bear was discovered in
          1899. The mountain gorilla wasn't
          known until 1901.

                    DEAN HAMPTON
          I'm not sure that's relevant.

                    LACY
          In 1975 a new species of shark
          was found. It is not outside of
          the realm of possibility, of
          possibility, that a K'ang Mi exists.
                    (passionate)
          It is that possibility that I'm
          teaching, that potential.

                    DEAN HAMPTON
          Well, stop.

Lacy turns away angrily, then just as quickly, turns
back, even more passionately. . . .

                    LACY
          Stop getting students interested?
          Stop getting them curious? Stop
          challenging them? You should have
          seen them turn on. It was electric.

Selling it more. Giving the protagonist expanded lines.

Dean Hampton studies her.

                    DEAN HAMPTON
          This is not the first complaint.

Shortened dialogue.

Lacy throws up her hands.

                    LACY
          I can't teach a curriculum I don't
          believe in.

After a beat . . .

>   DEAN HAMPTON
>   I guess that says it all.

She holds out her hand to shake.

>   DEAN HAMPTON
>   (continuing)
>   I'll get a replacement for you for
>   tomorrow's classes. I'm sorry it had
>   to end this way.

Lacy's stunned.

Dean Hampton shakes her hand.

>   DEAN HAMPTON
>   (continuing; distant)
>   I've enjoyed having you on the
>   faculty. Good luck.

And she spins and walks away.

Hand still out, Lacy is absolutely speechless.

>   DISSOLVE TO:

EXT. CHARLES RIVER - THAT NIGHT

The setting sun shining off the water.

INT. LACY'S APARTMENT - NIGHT

Sitting on the floor in front of the couch, holding a
beer, with the same shocked expression she had when
Dean Hampton fired her.

```
                                          DISSOLVE TO:


EXT. PUBLIC SCHOOL PARKING LOT - DAY

The double-breasted suit Lacy was wearing with Dean
Hampton is featured prominently on a rack in the
NEIGHBORHOOD TAG SALE of Lacy's stuff. Books, shoes,
kitchen items, what looks like Lacy's whole life
except for her computers,
```

```
books, and research, being picked over by neighbors
and bargain hunters in search for treasures.

A rushed
```

```
Lacy talks with WALTER, a man in jeans and a barn
coat.

                        LACY
              I really appreciate this. I just got
              paged. He doesn't have much time.

And she runs off.
```

INT. BOSTON HOSPITAL - WARD - LATER THAT DAY

A faded black-and-white photograph of Mt. Everest taped on the wall.

Lacy sits next to the hospital bed, tape recording an OLD TIBETAN, whose eyes are foggy white with blindness.

> OLD TIBETAN
> As boy, I was to Thyangboche and
> Pangboche with father. He showed me
> proof. . . .

The Old Tibetan puts his tired hand on Lacy's wrist. His skin is bronze and leathery.

> OLD TIBETAN
> He gave to museum New York
> City . . .

The Old Tibetan slowly opens his mouth wide . . . he
has no teeth . . . and points inside.

                    OLD TIBETAN
          . . . K'ang Mi.

Lacy tries to understand. The Old Tibetan points into
his mouth again, then . . .

                    OLD TIBETAN
                    (continuing)
          K'ang Mi.

                         LACY
          What?

Less detail. More mystery added.

The Old Tibetan's eyes close and breathing labors.
She touches his hand.

                         LACY
          Thank you.

EXT. NEW YORK CITY - HELICOPTER SHOT - DAY

Gliding over Central Park, over Central Park West to
the venerable old Museum of Natural History with
snaking lines of school kids climbing the steps and
hot dog vendors hawking their greasy wares.

Lacy rushes down windswept Central Park West, then
hurries up the steps of the museum and enters.

INT. MUSEUM LIBRARY - OFFICE - DAY

A digital display runs numbers and dates ends on
AUGUST 12, 1937, 5:00 P.M.

A YOUNG ASIAN MAN in a gray cotton jacket looks up
from the computer.

> YOUNG MAN
> We're digitized only as far back as
> August 12, 1937 . . . sorry.

INT. MUSEUM LIBRARY - STORAGE - LATER THAT DAY

Stuffed specimens in dusty display bell jars. Books
upon books. Old paper files.

Log books with faded green canvas covers.

Notations made in beautifully written nineteenth-
century ink curlicues.

Lacy uses a magnifying glass as she goes down the
long lists of objects logged into the museum's
collection.

Slightly expanded.

Rockin' to his Walkman, A YOUNG ASIAN MAN in a gray
cotton staff jacket enters.

Rewritten because of awkward writing. He's still inexplicably Asian.

```
              YOUNG MAN
      Dr. Kendricks, how long you gonna
```

Slanged.

```
      be here today?
```

Lacy smiles. She's tired.

```
                  LACY
      To the bitter end.
```

Rewritten dialogue. Trying to find the voice of the main character.

```
              YOUNG MAN
             (sympathetically)
      You want a soda, something?
```

Lacy holds up her thermos.

```
                  LACY
      Just keep all knives and sharp
      objects away from me, okay?

              YOUNG MAN
      What year you up to?
```

Lacy checks the cover of the book.

```
                  LACY
      1914.
```

New year.

>   YOUNG MAN
>   (lying badly)
>   Hey, you're movin' right along.

Lacy LAUGHS.

The Young Man smiles and walks out, his footsteps
ECHOING crisply on the shiny linoleum floors.

Lacy returns to the log book and goes down the list
of entries with the magnifying glass, which she puts
down, and with her eyes never leaving the log book,
unscrews the top of the thermos bottle and pours
herself the last of the hot tea.

As she's screwing on the top . . . she stops. Lacy puts
down the thermos and picks the magnifying glass back
up.

THROUGH THE MAGNIFYING GLASS

to the turn-of-the-century

Instead of nineteenth-century.

script:

One K'ang Mi incisor. 3.678 mm by 1.276 mm.

Thangboche Monastery. No. 45.612-AR.

Lacy can't believe her eyes.

No more London, remember?

INT. MUSEUM OF NATURAL HISTORY - DAY

Lacy paces in front of the research desk as the
portly DIRECTOR OF EXHIBITS returns holding a
yellowed item card.

> DIRECTOR
> I'm a tad embarrassed to say we
> actually don't know where 45.612-AR
> is. It's inexplicable, really. I
> have the card, but no 45.612-AR.

Revised, shorter dialogue. I don't miss London.

> LACY
> Then it's here . . . somewhere?

The Director looks the card over, then slowly nods.

> DIRECTOR
> That would be the indication . . .
> but as to precisely where . . .

The Director is at a loss.

New line. Deletion of Evan in the London Pub scene. Miss it? Miss that twit Evan?

INT. MUSEUM - SPECIMEN STORAGE - DAY

Boxes, crates, of all sizes, with every kind of
label, stacked a dozen deep nearly to the ceiling.

Lacy examines a small, tooth-sized, meticulously
crafted little wood crate.

With a small electric screwdriver, she unscrews the
six screws on one side and gently lifts off the crate
top.

Inside is Lacracean toricolethum, a horrifying-
looking specimen of a horned beetle which falls out
of the box, scaring her.

A jump moment. Even our hero can be scared.

After her initial surprise, disappointment.

Deletion of Evan and Lacy walk and talk. I don't miss it for a second.

INT. MUSEUM - SPECIMEN STORAGE - THE NEXT DAY

Another small crate. Lacy prying it open.

Inside, a nearly perfect quartz crystal. It glints in
the work lights. She's bummed.

She closes that box and picks up another. Lacy's
tired. There's no marking on the box of any kind.
Unable to squash her excitement, Lacy quickly forces
the box open.

Added description.

Inside is a single tiny bone . . . nothing.
Disappointed, Lacy closes the box.

INT. MUSEUM - SPECIMEN STORAGE - THE NEXT DAY

Lacy empties the last of the tea out of the thermos
and looks at the unopened stack of six dozen small
specimen cases.

She takes a deep tired breath, then grabs a small
screwdriver, pries open the unlabeled old crate,
unpacks the straw revealing . . .

. . . a stained incisor!

A glorious thing: shiny, worn, huge.

Lacy checks the faded scrawl and number on the item
card.

45.612-AR

Deletion of Latin. Slows script down.

She breaks into a broad smile.

Lacy lifts the incisor reverently out of the
box. . . . It's much bigger than a human tooth.

Deletion of another Evan scene. I've cut five pages so far from the draft. Stream-
lining. Making choices. Getting to it faster.

INT. MUSEUM - DATING LAB - DAY

A huge potassium/argon dater.

Two gray-smocked Technicians work on the controls.

Lacy watches with interest as the incisor is placed
on the titanium caddy.

It slides into the cage and the thick glass door
slides down.

The red light turns green.

Lacy watches from behind the control board.

The digital display reads <u>1400 A.D.</u>

Lacy gasps, then pumps her arm happily.

The Technician walks over to the ecstatic Lacy.

                    TECHNICIAN
          It's nearly contemporary.

                      LACY
          I know. I saw!

EXT. WASHINGTON, D.C. - DAY

The stodgy National Geographic Society's
headquarters.

INT. NATIONAL GEOGRAPHIC OFFICE - DAY

Ornate and filled with the exotic plunder of a
thousand expeditions.

Lacy sits in front of the ASSISTANT DIRECTOR'S
antique desk. He's midthirties, Ivy League, a bit
full of himself.

Deletion of overlong description.

                    ASSISTANT DIRECTOR
            Your project is very interesting,
            but, unfortunately, it falls a
            little below our radar.

Expanded dialogue.

She holds up a four-by-five color slide of the K'ang
Mi incisor.

                    LACY
            But I have proof.

New visual for scene.

He holds out his hand and smiles.

                    ASSISTANT DIRECTOR
            Here's one of my cards.

                    LACY
        If I'm right . . .

                        ASSISTANT DIRECTOR
            Then, please, give me a call.

New ending for scene.

EXT. EXPLORERS CLUB - DAY

The beaux arts center for adventurers.

Deletion of voice-over.

INT. EXPLORERS CLUB - HALLWAY - DAY

A large, cobwebbed

Changed from the more pedestrian "dusty."

buffalo head on the wall.

Lacy walks with COMMANDER PHILLIPS, a thin man with
an unfortunately drooping handlebar mustache and a
game left leg.

                    COMMANDER PHILLIPS
            We're really not in the bigfoot
            business . . . sorry.

New dialogue.

A disappointed Lacy shakes the Commander's hand and
exits unhappily.

EXT. NEW YORK CITY - DOWNTOWN LOFT - NIGHT

The setting sun reflects in the large industrial
windows.

Added word "setting" to make it more beautiful.

INT. MATTHEW HARDAWAY'S LOFT - NIGHT

Changed from day.

On a big-screen TV monitor: More of the black-and-white
Chinese film of the man/beasts hunting in the snow.

                    LACY'S VOICE
          This next piece is optically blown
          up.

BLACK AND WHITE

Very grainy and hard to make out. Reminiscent of the
satellite blow-up footage. Barely silhouettes, they
don't look human, but they also don't look like any
recognizable animal.

The return of the footage from the tease.

                    LACY'S VOICE
          This is supposedly early Chinese
          footage. The titles say it was shot
          in 1921.

                    HARDAWAY'S VOICE
          It could have been faked.

LACY'S VOICE
It's been analyzed. Everyone says
it's authentic.

The hunters have their prey and are violently
stabbing it to death.

New visuals to make it more interesting. Should probably make more of it.

Black screen.

The lights come on. Hardaway's loft is huge and
minimal. White walls. A few pieces of world-class
art. Lots of computers and monitors. Art deco
furniture and MATTHEW HARDAWAY.

HARDAWAY
Very cool.

Midthirties, expensively dressed in a Brooks Brothers
button-down shirt, pressed jeans, and barefoot,
Hardaway hands Lacy an orange juice and walks to the
table covered with maps of the Himalayas, large color
slides of the incisor from all angles, drawings of the
man/beasts.

Lacy watches him. Hardaway checks the map of Bhutan.

Deletion of him offering her a drink. More bad stuff.

HARDAWAY
How many days do you see the
expedition taking?

>   LACY
>   Once we're in Bhutan, it'll take
>   three days to get to Mount Chomo
>   Lhari, then . . .
>   (smiling)
>   . . . who knows.

Hardaway nods as he continues to look over Lacy's
materials.

Lacy walks over to the window and the view uptown of
Manhattan's lights coming on. She turns back to him as
he looks over the color slides of the K'ang Mi incisor.

>   LACY
>   I've budgeted the expedition at a
>   million dollars.

Hardaway is unfazed.

>   HARDAWAY
>   And if you find something?

Lacy doesn't understand the question.

>   HARDAWAY
>   (continuing)
>   Let's say the expedition finds this
>   K'ang Mi, who owns it?

Lacy studies him.

                    LACY
          No one owns anyone else.

His eyes blink with thought as he studies her.

Lacy looks right in his eyes.

                    LACY
                 (continuing)
          There's a chance to make history
          here.

I lost the "first great adventure of new century." It was a little much.

After a long moment . . .

                    HARDAWAY
          I'll have papers drawn up.

Lacy can't believe it. She holds out her hand.

                    LACY
          We have a deal?

                    HARDAWAY
          Deal.

He gives her a hug . . . and holds it a little too
long.

This is all that's left of Hardaway hitting on Lacy. Now it's a hint.

Lacy laughs in happy disbelief as she gently pulls
away from him.

                    HARDAWAY
          The publicity alone is worth more
          than a million.

But Hardaway's not finished.

                    HARDAWAY
                  (continuing)
          It has to be called the Hardaway
          Expedition.

Lacy's taken by surprise. After a beat . . .

New description.

                    LACY
          OK.

                    HARDAWAY
          The find has to be called Hardaway
          Man.

She looks at him for even a longer beat.

                    LACY
          I'm not sure . . .

                    HARDAWAY
                  (interrupting)
          And I go along on the expedition.

New ending to scene follows . . .

Lacy looks at him in disbelief.

Hardaway holds the color slide up to the light.

> HARDAWAY
> Those terms are nonnegotiable.

>> CUT TO:

EXT. THE HIMALAYAS - DAY

The staggering sun-bathed snowy crest of the Himalayas towers over the tiny green Buddhist kingdom
of Bhutan. BUDDHIST TRANCE MUSIC plays.

New description. This is seventeen pages. Things are happening faster and we
get into the heart of the script sooner. I've cut eight pages so far. So that means
you get to read eight new pages. I go back to first-draft smart-alecky notes.

EXT. THE PARO VALLEY - DAY - MUSIC CONTINUES

A verdant valley of Buddhist temples, fields with
herds of yak, and the occasional stone farmhouse.

In a centuries-old outbuilding, a shiny red Chinese
tractor.

I've actually been to Bhutan and am using those firsthand experiences as my
research.

EXT. PARO - DAY - MUSIC CONTINUES

A small town of low-slung ancient white buildings and
old people in maroon and orange highly decorated
indigenous garb.

The occasional TV satellite dish on a roof is the
only object that distinguishes it from the 1890s.
Until . . .

EXT. PARO AIRPORT - DAY

The THWACKING THROB of a cargo helicopter emblazoned
with HARDAWAY EXPEDITION on the side hovers down to a
landing.

Another THROBBING helicopter drops down and lands
nearby.

The first one on the ground is already being unloaded
of high-tech plastic crates labeled HARDAWAY
EXPEDITION. Everything is being covered by two
frantic VIDEOGRAPHERS and a STILL CAMERAWOMAN.

New stuff. New characters. New location. Lots of energy. Reenergizes the script
and the reader/viewer.

INT. HANGAR - DAY - DOCUMENTARY VIDEO

Filled with ropes, pitons, dried-food packages, and
mountaineering and electronic equipment. More sleek
plastic cases labeled HARDAWAY EXPEDITION.

Detailed topographical maps and computer printouts
pinned to the wall. A red line is drawn from Paro to
the summit of Chomo Lhari.

SUTTON, forty, in canvas pants, a down vest, climbing
boots, and a quarter-inch buzz cut, lights a
cigarette, takes a deep drag, then . . .

                    SUTTON
           (sullenly answering a question)
         Lew Sutton. I've lived in these
         mountains, mostly Nepal, for the
         last fifteen, twenty years.

INT. HANGAR - DAY

Sutton looks directly into the video camera held by
the young Videographer.

                    SUTTON
         And just to go on the record. I
         don't believe there's a K'ang Mi or
         any . . .
           (barely able to keep a straight face)
         . . . "man/beast of the Himalayas"
         up there. No big deal.

                    VIDEOGRAPHER
         And your job is?

                    SUTTON
         Chief guide.

INT. HANGAR - DAY - VIDEO

The Videographer PANS to a laughing JAMES, twenty-
one, buffed to the extreme, taking snapshots of the
videographer shooting him, then lowering his camera.

                    JAMES
            (into camera)
         I'm James Devine. And I'm real
         excited to be part of this whole
                    (more)

                    JAMES (cont'd)
          thing. I've done a lot of climbing:
          Everest, Annapurna, Patagonia. My
          job is logistics and support. I
          wrangle the satellite location
          system.

INT. HANGAR - DAY

James looks to his left to GABY, a beautiful, very
athletic woman, twenty-three, who smiles at the video
camera.

                    GABY
                (French accent)
          My name is Gabriella Probert, Gaby
          is what they call me. I was on the
          '97 Italian climb of Everest. Officer
          Medicale. My English it is not so
          good, so please be patience with me.

She smiles a warm smile and looks to her left.

INT. HANGAR - DAY - VIDEO

PIRU, under five feet, indeterminate age, maybe
thirty, probably sixty, with a knowing smile,
uncomfortable with a camera on him.

                    PIRU
          I Piru. From Bhutan. I have climb
          Chomo Lhari . . . never north face.
          No one ever climb north face. I have
          not seen snow demon, but . . .
                (after a beat,
                a smile, then)
          I Piru.

INT. HANGAR - DAY

Resplendent in his custom expedition-ware and
<u>HARDAWAY EXPEDITION</u> down jacket, Hardaway claps Piru
on the shoulder.

> HARDAWAY
> "Snow Demon." Good name. I'm
> Hardaway-dot-com. You've probably
> heard of the Hardaway Group of
> companies. I'm funding the Hardaway
> Expedition . . .
> > (smiling)
> . . . Matthew Hardaway.
> > (looking around)
> I can't thank you all enough for
> participating. And the reason we're
> all here . . .
> > (looking to his left)
> Dr. Lacy Kendricks.

Everyone smiles and APPLAUDS.

Lacy blushes.

> LACY
> Thanks . . . I hope we're all
> applauding as much when we come down
> off the mountain.

> HARDAWAY
> We will be.

                         LACY
      I'm Lacy.
                    (smiling)
      The bottom line is: the buck stops
      here . . .
                    (pointing to herself)
      . . . with me, about everything.

Lacy lets that sink in.

Sutton glances over at Hardaway, who hasn't changed
expression.

                         LACY
                    (continuing)
      We are climbing Mount Chomo Lhari,
      which, I'm sure you all know, is a
      holy mountain, one of the Himalayan
      deities.

Piru nods knowingly.

                         LACY
                    (continuing)
      We must treat her with the utmost
      respect. No drinking, drugs, sexual
      activity, nothing that can be
      considered negative or insulting in
      any way toward the mountain.
      Anything else, Piru?

Piru allows himself a missing-some-teeth smile.

                         PIRU
      The mountain forgives Westerners.

Lacy smiles at Piru, then turns to the others.

                    LACY
          My hope, for all of us, is that
          Chomo Lhari will give up its secrets.

                  HARDAWAY
          Does anyone have anything to say or
          any questions?

                    SUTTON
              (to the videographers)
          You guys ever done any climbing?

     One of the videographers lowers his digital video
     camera and shakes his head. The other as well.

     Obstacles again.

     Sutton winces.

                    SUTTON
              Suicide.

                  HARDAWAY
          We need a record.

                    SUTTON
          You'll have a record of people dying
          on the mountain.

                  HARDAWAY
          It's my decision.

                    LACY
          Matthew, Sutton's correct. We're on
          the edge up here . . . as strong as
                    (more)

                    LACY (cont'd)
          our weakest link and
          nonclimbers. . . .

She shakes her head.

                    LACY
                 (continuing)
          I've climbed, everyone but you has.
          Three more who haven't doesn't make
          sense.

Hardaway, tense, finally nods his agreement.

                    HARDAWAY
          We have still cameras.

                    JAMES
          I'll be shooting.

                    HARDAWAY
          OK, no video.

                    LACY
          Great. Six A.M. tomorrow morning.
          Rain or shine.

Everyone looks at each other. They're nervous and
excited.

Lacy puts her hand up in the air over her head.

Gaby puts hers alongside Lacy's.

James does as well.

                    HARDAWAY
          Yeah.

And he puts his hand with the others.

Finally, Sutton reluctantly joins them and they're a
team.

                                              CUT TO:

EXT. BHUTAN - DAY

The peaks covered with clouds.

EXT. MOUNTAIN TRAIL - DAY

Bhutanese shepherds dressed in the native <u>saros,</u>
skirtlike affairs, walk with their yak along the
well-worn paths.

The two THUMPING <u>HARDAWAY EXPEDITION</u> helicopters
fly low, spooking the yak as they head up to Mount
Chomo Lhari.

INT. HELICOPTER - DAY

Flying low over the wilderness. Piru looks very
unhappy in the corner. Lacy sits in the other corner
with Hardaway.

                    HARDAWAY
          When we were in New York, I thought
          I felt something between us.

Lacy waits for more.

                    HARDAWAY
                  (continuing)
          Was I wrong?

                    LACY
          A different time and different
          place.

                    HARDAWAY
          I believe in you.

Lucy LAUGHS and blushes.

                    HARDAWAY
                  (continuing)
          What?

                    LACY
          The way you say "I believe in you"
          sounds like "I want to sleep with
          you."

Hardaway studies her a second.

                    HARDAWAY
          I know you're not with anyone.

                    LACY
          How do? . . .

She doesn't finish. Hardaway smiles a little self-
consciously.

                    HARDAWAY
          I like to know who I'm in business
          with.

> LACY
> Then it shouldn't come as much of a
> surprise to you that I'm
> saying . . .
>> (after a beat)
> . . . thanks, but no thanks. It's
> very flattering, but . . .
>> (LAUGHING gently)
> I'm really busy . . . with all
> this. . . .

Hardaway understands, but Lacy senses he hasn't
really signed off on it yet.

> LACY
>> (continuing)
> It's unprofessional,
> counterproductive, and totally out
> of the question. Clear enough?

Gaby's checking medical supplies.

Lacy walks past Sutton and James.

> JAMES
> She's a pretty amazing woman.

Sutton puts an unlit cigarette in his mouth.

> SUTTON
> Don't waste your time.

> JAMES
> I mean her work.

> SUTTON
> You would.

EXT. MOUNTAINSIDE - SUNSET

The THROBBING choppers on the ground, their propellers still spinning.

The Westerners are around the fire drinking tea, arguing.

> HARDAWAY
> They can take us higher, save time.

Lacy shakes her head.

> LACY
> Piru says the mountain doesn't like
> the noisy birds.

Hardaway looks over at the guides crouching in a circle, passing around yak butter and talking and chuckling under their breath. Piru averts his eyes.

Hardaway turns back to Lacy.

> HARDAWAY
> These guys are like out of the
> fifteenth century. What do they know?

> LACY
> They know the mountain.

Hardaway thinks for a moment, then shakes his head.

<pre>
                    HARDAWAY
          Unbelievable.

He lifts his radio.

                    HARDAWAY
            (continuing; into the radio)
          OK, let 'em go.

The helicopters REV UP and chopper off the mountain
leaving the hillside dotted with colorful poly tents
and the expedition.

Hardaway looks around.

It's staggering . . . and silent except for the ever-
present WIND.

They're alone.

The wind picks up and starts HOWLING across the face
of the mountain . . . it's eerie.
</pre>

Now the rewrites are a lot about maximizing and perfecting. Of course, the problem is there is no one right way to write. There are a lot of ways to solve the creative problem in a scene. Therefore, theoretically, you could rewrite forever. Making changes. Making it different.

The following pages were part of the draft I sent out to buyers in Hollywood.

<u>**K'ANG MI**</u>
<u>**THE THIRD DRAFT**</u>

Written by Tom Lazarus

FADE IN:

BLACK SCREEN

Jumpy white titles in <u>Chinese.</u> WIND BLOWING.

BLACK AND WHITE - WIND CONTINUES

Old film footage of the Himalayas, crudely cut together,
slightly speeded up, of the sunset glaring off the snow.

BLACK AND WHITE - WIND CONTINUES

In the distance, running jerkily, three large figures,
loping really, appear to be carrying large sticks.

The images are blurry and handheld, hard to make out,
as the light fades.

The figures run faster . . . they're chasing
something . . .

. . . something smaller . . .

. . . something running in fear.

BLACK AND WHITE - WIND CONTINUES

TELEPHOTO. Even less light. CLOSE UP of the figures in
blurry silhouette . . .

. . . thrashing around, fighting . . .

. . . violent, animalistic . . .

. . . murderous.

Stretching out this moment for more impact.

                                                    CUT TO:

BLACK SCREEN

The CLICK and CHUGS of a computer processing . . .

More description.

FADE IN:

INT. UNIVERSITY DIGITAL LAB - NIGHT - MAIN TITLES

Two silhouetted figures, a man and a woman, in front
of a wall-size digital monitor showing Earth from a
photography satellite.

                         MAN'S VOICE
               This is from Comsat 104.

ON DIGITAL MONITOR

A hemispheric slice closer.

                         WOMAN'S VOICE
                         (continuing)
               We're looking for longitude 92.2
               degrees east by latitude 27.3
               degrees north.

ON DIGITAL MONITOR

The north Indian/Chinese/Russian landmass with a
storm twisting out of the Indian Ocean.

ON THE MAN

He's ALLAN, out-of-date sideburns, striped shirt and
tie. Very focused and unaware of his nerdiness.

                    ALLAN
          What kind of magnification are you
          looking for?

ON THE WOMAN

She's DR. LACY KENDRICKS, thirties, as beautiful as
she is brilliant, much more intense than Allan, much
more alive and energized, in a turtleneck with a
flannel shirt over it, jeans, hiking boots, and into
it . . . big-time.

                    LACY
          To the wall. Go for it!

Allan smiles and types instructions into the
computer.

ON DIGITAL MONITOR

ZOOMING IN on northern India.

Individual characteristics become visible. Mountains,
plains, snaking rivers reflecting the ruthless sun.

TIGHTER on Tibet, then Bhutan, the heart of the
Himalayas.

Lacy smiles.

ON DIGITAL MONITOR

CLOSER ON the craggy, snow-covered mountains of
Bhutan.

Lacy's blown away.

Allan smiles at Lacy's excitement.

ON DIGITAL MONITOR

The Chomo Lhari mountain range. Vast and dangerous.
The photographic grain is now blown up, forming
abstract patterns.

An ID of Chomo Lhari.

Lacy studying the monitor intensely.

The image searches . . .

> LACY'S VOICE
> I don't see anything.

> ALLAN'S VOICE
> Let me try the spectroscopic filter.

Allan types in commands.

The image changes. It's a field of grainy, multicolor
splotches.

Lacy leaps out of her seat.

>   LACY
>   There!

Allan doesn't see it.

Lacy rushes to the monitor and points to a spot on the
screen.

>   LACY
>   (continuing)
>   There!

Her finger points to a single green spot, just one
grain in a pointillist field of fuzzy dots.

>   LACY
>   (continuing)
>   That's it!

He turns to her, then, finally almost reluctantly . . .

>   ALLAN
>   It is _something._

Lacy lights up.

>   LACY
>   Proof!

>   ALLAN
>   It could be an artifact of the lens,
>   in transmission. . . .

Allan's not so sure.

TITLES END

EXT. EMERSON COLLEGE, BOSTON - DAY

Stark modern additions to the old campus in the
golden autumn sunlight as leaves blow past the
students walking between classes.

Book bag over her shoulder and scarf blowing behind
her, Lacy runs across the campus.

                    LACY'S VOICE
          My theory is . . .

Shortened dialogue.

INT. COLLEGE LECTURE HALL - DAY

A seminar class of fifty semi-interested
undergraduates sitting in the streamlined, sun-filled
room. Pacing back and forth, Lacy lectures . . .

                    LACY'S VOICE
                    (continuing)
          . . . that high in this remote
          Himalayan mountain range, there's a
          valley, sheltered from the harsh
          elements.

Dialogue added here.

The fuzzy dots with the greenish one in the center,
projected on the video screen.

                    LACY
                 (passionate)
          This valley could be home to what
          the Bhutanese call K'ang Mi, the
          legendary man/beast of the
          Himalayas.

An electric charge goes through the students.

Lacy smiles.

A student's hand thrusts into the air.

                    STUDENT
          Are you talking about the abominable
          snowman?

Lacy sits on the table.

                    LACY
          There is more than ample evidence
          that man/beasts, K'ang Mi,
          abominable snowmen, Sasquatch, yeti,
          call them what you will, roam many
          of the wilderness areas of the
          world.

Reversed this and the following dialogue. Which should come first?

The students are fascinated. At the back of the
class, an Asian student makes copious notes.

> LACY
>
> If the K'ang Mi does exist, it
> would offer a new way to interpret
> heretofore ambiguous
> paleoanthropological evidence.
> Hominid fossils once thought to be
> from the Middle Pleistocene or
> older periods may, in fact, be
> quite recent.

CLASS BELL.

Not a student jumps out of their seat.

A pleased Lacy smiles.

> LACY
> (continuing)
> We'll continue on Monday.

Lacy gathers her lecture notes as the class, BUZZING,
exits. The note-taking Asian student is among the
last to leave.

EXT. CHARLES RIVER, BOSTON - NIGHT

Through storm clouds, the full moon shines across the
water.

A thirty-story apartment tower overlooking the river.
The wind blows cold off the water . . . sounding
almost like an ANIMAL'S CRY.

On the twenty-fifth floor, a single light burns.

> Used to be twelfth floor. The reason for the change? Taller, better view. Better film. More special. Closer to God. Totally arbitrary.

                    ERIC SHIPTON'S VOICE
             I have just a second before my
             flight.

INT. TWENTY-FIFTH-FLOOR APARTMENT - NIGHT

Great view. One thousand square feet.

> Used to be four hundred square feet. Bigger. Easier to shoot. More impressive. I'm cranking this stuff up. Everything is important.

                    LACY'S VOICE
             What altitude?

On the wall behind the computer monitor, folk
drawings of man/beasts labeled <u>FEIFEI</u> from China and
<u>BATUTUT</u> from Borneo and <u>KAKUNDARI</u> and <u>KILOMBA</u> from
the Congo. A photograph of an exhilarated Lacy on top
of a snow-covered mountain.

> Added mountain-climbing photo of Lacy to make climb more real.

                    ERIC SHIPTON'S VOICE
             About eighteen thousand feet, on the
             Menlung glacier. There were two sets
             of footprints in the snow.

> Slightly shortened dialogue.

In sweats and running shoes, Lacy sits at her
keyboard, fascinated, taking notes.

                    LACY
          I've seen the photographs. Very
          persuasive.

On the computer screen, ERIC SHIPTON, an Australian
in his thirties, talks into CAMERA. He types on his
computer.

                  ERIC SHIPTON
          We did a computer extrapolation,
          based on weight and displacement
          variables.

ON MONITOR

A rotating computer-generated 3-D hologram of a
large, biped mammal, a cross between a man and a
bear.

                K'ANG MI PROJECTIONS

HEIGHT: 8' 2.5"

WEIGHT: 389 LBS.

STRENGTH TO AVERAGE HUMAN - 165.54%

SPEED FOR 100 METERS - 10.145 SECONDS.

Lacy is blown away, then . . .

                    LACY
          But you didn't see? . . .

Shipton shakes his head.

                    SHIPTON
          Unfortunately, we didn't see a
          thing, sorry. Gotta go.

Added dialogue.

                    LACY
          Thanks.

And Shipton's signal cuts out.

Lacy continues to make notes.

                    MAN'S VOICE
          I'm going to split.

Lacy climbs out of her chair and moves to the bed
where BRADLEY, midthirties, putting on his glasses,
is getting out of bed.

Introduction of major new character. The return of Evan in different form. (When I read this a few years after writing it, I thought it was probably a mistake. We'll see.)

                    LACY
          I had to get him before he got on a
          plane. Sorry.

Bradley, in his boxers, is putting on his pants.

                    LACY
                (continuing)
          I said I was sorry.

                    BRADLEY
          You're always sorry.

Lacy sags and sits on the bed.

                    LACY
          What do you want me to do, give up
          my research, stop searching, stop
          believing?

Bradley pulls on his socks.

                    LACY
                (continuing)
          I finally am going to meet this
          Tibetan who says he knows of proof,
          proof, of the K'ang Mi and you want
          me to walk away from it?

On the nose. Spelling it out. Not so sure of it.

Bradley is tying his shoe.

                    BRADLEY
          Time's running out.

Lacy nods. She knows.

                    LACY
          The doctors gave him a week two
          weeks ago.

Bradley pulls on his shirt.

                    BRADLEY
          I'm talking about your biological
          clock, I'm talking about us . . .
                    (disappointed)
          . . . and you're talking about the
          K'ang Mi. What a surprise.

                    LACY
          What do you want me to do?

Bradley buttons his shirt.

                    BRADLEY
          I'm too far down your list of
          priorities, having a family is too
          far down your list, you and me are
          too far down the list.

I like that gender issues are a little askew.

He heads toward the door.

                    LACY
          It doesn't help walking out.

Bradley stops and turns back to her.

                    BRADLEY
          OK, let's talk. Go.

The PHONE RINGS.

                    LACY
          I . . . I think we're going
          through . . .

The PHONE RINGS again.

> LACY
> (continuing)
> . . . a down time. Hold on, let me
> get this. . . .

Bradley shakes his head.

> LACY
> (continuing)
> It might be the hospital.
> > (answering the phone)
> Hi, it's Lacy.

A new way into the Dean.

INT. DEAN HAMPTON'S OFFICE - NIGHT

A troubled DEAN STEPHANIE HAMPTON, midforties, stern, behind her desk, talking on the phone.

> DEAN HAMPTON
> It's Dean Hampton. We have a
> problem.

The note-taking Asian Student watches the Dean on the phone.

INT. TWENTY-FIFTH-FLOOR APARTMENT - NIGHT

Lacy listening to the Dean on the phone, then . . .

> LACY
> I'll see you first thing in the
> morning. Thanks.

She hangs up and turns back to Bradley.

                    LACY
                (continuing)
          Brad . . .

But he's gone. She moves to the chair where Bradley's
clothes were and sits down. She looks at her dresser
where, in a sleek wood frame, there's a photograph of
her and Bradley kidding around. Happier times.

All new Bradley stuff. I'm still feeling a need for a human story. Not sure this is it.

EXT. EMERSON COLLEGE - ADMINISTRATION BUILDING - DAY

In her serious college-instructor double-breasted
suit, Lacy exits with Dean Hampton and they walk down
the tree-lined pathway. Dean Hampton is troubled.

                    DEAN HAMPTON
          Lacy, you're teaching anthropology,
          not science fiction.

Simpler dialogue.

They stop as they reach the large pigeon-stained
statue of the founder, Dunkirk Emerson, standing with
a walking stick in one hand and an open book in the
other.

                    LACY
          The Kodiak bear was discovered in
          1899. The mountain gorilla in 1901.

> DEAN HAMPTON
> I'm not sure that's relevant.

> LACY
> In 1975 a new species of shark was
> found. It is not outside the realm
> of possibility, of _possibility,_ that
> a K'ang Mi exists.
> (passionate)
> It is _that_ possibility that I'm
> teaching, that _potential._

> DEAN HAMPTON
> Well, stop.

Lacy turns away angrily, then just as quickly, turns back, even more passionately. . . .

> LACY
> Stop getting the students curious?
> Stop challenging them? You should
> have seen them turn on. You could
> feel the electricity.

Dean Hampton studies her.

> DEAN HAMPTON
> This is not the first complaint.

Lacy throws up her hands.

> LACY
> I can't teach a curriculum I don't
> believe in.

Dean Hampton shrugs.

                    DEAN HAMPTON
          I guess that says it all.

She holds out her hand to shake.

                    DEAN HAMPTON
                    (continuing)
          I'm sorry it had to end this way.

Lacy's stunned.

                    LACY
          "End"?

New dialogue for our protagonist. Keeps her in the scene.

                    DEAN HAMPTON
          No teacher, no matter how good, is
          bigger than the program.

Dean Hampton shakes her hand.

                    DEAN HAMPTON
                    (continuing; distant)
          I've enjoyed having you on the
          faculty. Good luck.

And she spins and walks away.

Hand still out, Lacy is absolutely speechless.

                                        DISSOLVE TO:

EXT. CHARLES RIVER - THAT NIGHT

The setting sun shining off the water.

New Bradley scene follows.

INT. LACY'S APARTMENT - NIGHT

Sitting on the floor in front of the couch, holding a
beer, with the same shocked expression she had with
Dean Hampton. Bradley, angry, is pacing.

                    BRADLEY
          You were on tenure track for
          chrissakes. You couldn't just suck
          it up, just once, and gone along
          with the program?

Lacy looks at him as if he were speaking a foreign
language.

                    LACY
          No, actually, I couldn't.

                    BRADLEY
          I guess I just don't get it.

After a beat, Lacy nods.

                    LACY
          I was thinking exactly that.

Bradley looks at her for a moment, then . . .

                    BRADLEY
                 (barely audible)
          I'm going.

Lacy nods.

And Bradley walks out.

Lacy stands, moves to the window and looks out over the lights twinkling along the Charles and fights to control her emotions . . . but can't, as the tears brim out of her eyes.

> More of a scene. More emotion. More conflict. Less ties: no school. No more reasons for her not to go for it. More for the actress to do. And Bradley's gone. He served his purpose.

                                        CUT TO:

EXT. PUBLIC SCHOOL PARKING LOT - DAY

The double-breasted suit Lacy was wearing with Dean Hampton is featured prominently on a rack in the NEIGHBORHOOD TAG SALE of Lacy's stuff.

Books, shoes, kitchen items, the sleek wooden frame without the photograph of Lacy and Bradley, what looks like Lacy's whole life except for her computers, books, and research, being picked over by neighbors and bargain hunters in search of treasures.

Lacy talks with BECCA, an Asian woman about Lacy's age, in jeans and a barn coat.

> Becca is a new character. She's Asian. I'm apparently going for an all-Asian supporting cast. Inexplicable.

                    LACY
          I can't ignore what's going on
          around me. . . .

                    BECCA
          And Bradley?

A new part of the Bradley line.

Lacy makes a face.

                    LACY
          He played the biological clock card.

                    BECCA
          He wasn't the one.

Lacy shakes her head.

                    LACY
          Close, but no cigar.

Becca smiles.

                    BECCA
          Well, if he doesn't have a
          cigar . . .

And they both LAUGH . . . suddenly, Lacy yanks her
beeper out of her pocket and looks at it.

                    LACY
          Oh, God, it's the hospital. . . .

Cranking up the drama.

                              BECCA
                    Go, go . . . I'll do this.

Lacy runs for her car. . . .

                              LACY
                         (over her shoulder)
                    Thanks!

                              BECCA
                    For ten percent!

But Lacy's gone.

INT. BOSTON HOSPITAL - WARD - LATER THAT DAY

The blinds are closed. Monitors BEEP and CLICK
nearby.

New, dramatic way to get into scene.

Lacy sits next to the hospital bed videotaping a
fading OLD TIBETAN, whose eyes are foggy white with
blindness. His voice is weak and labored. . . .

More detailed scene description. Now there's a time clock: This guy's going to
croak.

                         OLD TIBETAN
                    As boy, I went Thyangboche Temple
                    with Father. He showed me proof of
                    K'ang Mi. . . .

Lacy moves her chair closer.

                    LACY
        What proof?

The Old Tibetan puts his tired hand, an IV taped to
his transparent skin, on Lacy's wrist. . . .

                  OLD TIBETAN
            He give to Natural History Museum
            New York City . . .

Excited, Lacy leans forward.

                    LACY
                  (gently)
            Yes. What did he give them?

The Old Tibetan slowly opens his mouth wide . . . he
has no teeth . . . and points inside.

                  OLD TIBETAN
            . . . K'ang Mi.

Lacy smiles, tries to understand. The Old Tibetan
points into his mouth again, then . . .

                  OLD TIBETAN
                  (continuing)
        K'ang Mi.

Lacy leans closer to whisper in his ear. . . .

                    LACY
            I don't understand. What proof?

The Old Tibetan's breathing labors. She tenderly
caresses his hand.

                              LACY
                           (continuing)
                    Thank you so much. . . .

And the old Tibetan's eyes close and his breathing
evens.

An expanded scene which gives more information in a more streamlined fashion.

EXT. NEW YORK CITY - HELICOPTER SHOT - DAY

The skyline, gliding over the meadow in Central Park,
over Central Park West to the venerable Museum of
Natural History with lines of school kids snaking up
the steps and hot dog vendors hawking their greasy
wares.

Slightly expanded, and when I read it a couple of years later, not as good.

Lacy hurries up the steps of the museum and enters.

Slightly cut.

INT. MUSEUM LIBRARY - OFFICE - DAY

A digital display runs numbers and dates and stops on
AUGUST 12, 1937, 5:00 P.M.

A YOUNG ASIAN MAN in a gray cotton jacket looks up
from the computer.

                        YOUNG MAN
                 We're digitized only as far back as
                 August 12, 1937 . . . sorry.

INT. MUSEUM LIBRARY - LATER THAT DAY

Stuffed specimens in dusty display bell jars. Books
upon books. Old paper files.

Leather-bound log books with faded canvas covers.

On the green-striped yellowed pages, notations made
in beautifully written nineteenth-century ink
curlicues.

Lacy uses a magnifying glass as she goes down the
long lists of objects logged into the museum's
collection.

Rockin' to his Walkman, a young Asian Man enters.

                    YOUNG MAN
          Dr. Kendricks, how long you gonna be
          here today?

Lacy smiles. She's tired.

                    LACY
          Right up to the bitter end.

                    YOUNG MAN
                 (sympathetically)
          You want a soda, something?

Lacy holds up her thermos.

                    LACY
          Just keep all knives and sharp
          objects away from me, okay?

                    YOUNG MAN
          What year you up to?

Lacy checks the cover of the book.

                         LACY
          1914.

                    YOUNG MAN
                  (lying badly)
          Hey, you're movin' right along.

Lacy LAUGHS.

The Young Man smiles and walks out, his footsteps
ECHOING crisply on the shiny linoleum floors.

Lacy returns to the log book and goes down the list
of entries with her magnifying glass, which she puts
down, and with her eyes never leaving the log book,
unscrews the top of the thermos bottle and pours
herself the last of the hot tea.

As she's screwing the top back on, Lacy stops.

She puts down the thermos and picks up the magnifying
glass.

THROUGH THE MAGNIFYING GLASS

to the turn-of-the-century script:

No. 45.612-AR.

One K'ang Mi incisor. 3.678 mm by 1.276 mm.

Thyangboche Monastery, Bhutan, 10.4.14

Lacy can't believe her eyes. It's a tooth!

INT. MUSEUM OF NATURAL HISTORY - RESEARCH - DAY

Excited,

Lacy paces in front of the research desk as the portly DIRECTOR OF EXHIBITS returns holding a yellowed item card.

> DIRECTOR
> I'm a tad embarrassed to say we
> actually don't know where 45.612-AR
> is. It's inexplicable, really. I
> have the card, but no 45.612-AR.

> LACY
> Then it's here . . . somewhere?

The Director looks the card over, then slowly nods.

> DIRECTOR
> That would be the indication . . .
> but as to precisely where . . .

> LACY
> And if I were to look?

                              DIRECTOR
              We have . . .
                         (sheepish)
              . . . thirty-five million specimens.

INT. MUSEUM - SPECIMEN STORAGE - DAY

Boxes, crates, of all sizes, none with labels,
stacked a dozen deep nearly to the ceiling.

Lacy examines a small, tooth-sized, meticulously
crafted, little wood crate.

With a small electric screwdriver, she unscrews the
four screws on one side and gently lifts off the crate
top.

Inside is <u>Lacracerian toricolethum,</u> a horrifying-
looking specimen of horned beetle.

After her initial surprise, disappointment.

INT. MUSEUM - SPECIMEN STORAGE - THE NEXT DAY

Another small crate.

There's no marking on the box of any kind. Unable to
squash her excitement, Lacy quickly forces the box
open.

Inside is a single tiny bone . . . nothing.

Defeated, Lacy closes the box.

INT. MUSEUM - SPECIMEN STORAGE - THE NEXT DAY

Lacy empties the last of the tea out of the thermos
and looks at the unopened stack of six dozen small,
unlabeled specimen cases.

Shortened slightly.

She takes a deep tired breath, then grabs a small
screwdriver, pries open the old crate, unpacks the
straw revealing . . .

Shortened slightly.

. . . a stained incisor!

A glorious thing: shiny, worn, huge.

Lacy checks the faded scrawl and number on the
specimen card.

45.612-AR

She breaks into a broad smile.

Lacy lifts the incisor reverently out of the
box . . . it's much bigger than a human tooth.

INT. MUSEUM - DATING LAB - DAY

A high-tech potassium/argon dater.

Two gray-smocked TECHNICIANS work on the control
board.

Lacy watches as the incisor is placed on the titanium
caddy.

It slides into the cage and the thick safety glass
door SNAPS shut.

The red light turns green.

Lacy watches from behind the control board.

The digital display floats, then stops at <u>1600 A.D.</u>

Lacy GASPS, then pumps her arm happily.

The Technician walks over to the ecstatic Lacy.

                    TECHNICIAN
          It's nearly contemporary.

                    LACY
          I know. I saw!

EXT. WASHINGTON, D.C. - DAY

The stodgy National Geographic Society's
headquarters.

INT. NATIONAL GEOGRAPHIC OFFICE - DAY

Ornate and filled with the exotic plunder of a
thousand expeditions.

Lacy sits in front of the ASSISTANT DIRECTOR'S
antique desk. He's midthirties, Ivy League, a bit
full of himself.

> ASSISTANT DIRECTOR
> Your project is very interesting,
> but, unfortunately, it falls a
> little below our radar.

She holds up a four-by-five color slide of the
K'ang Mi incisor.

> LACY
> I had the tooth examined by experts.
> They said it definitely wasn't human,
> but they couldn't say what animal
> it's from . . . which was very, very
> encouraging. They tried to get DNA
> from it, but it was too degraded.

New dialogue. More for the protagonist to do.

> ASSISTANT DIRECTOR
> Here's one of my cards. . . .

> LACY
> And if I'm right?

The Assistant smiles.

                    ASSISTANT DIRECTOR
              Then, please, give us a call.

EXT. EXPLORERS CLUB - DAY

The beaux arts center for adventurers.

INT. EXPLORERS CLUB - HALLWAY - DAY

A large, cobwebbed buffalo head on the wall.

Lacy walks with COMMANDER PHILLIPS, a thin man with a
game left leg.

> Lost the handlebar mustache description.

                    COMMANDER PHILLIPS
              We're really not in the Bigfoot
              business . . . sorry.

> New dialogue. Moved from deleted Explorer's Club scene.

A disappointed Lacy shakes the Commander's hand and
exits unhappily.

EXT. NEW YORK CITY - DOWNTOWN LOFT - NIGHT

The setting sun reflects in the large industrial
windows of a gentrified turn-of-the-century warehouse.

> More specific description.

INT. MATTHEW HARDAWAY'S LOFT - NIGHT

On a big-screen TV monitor: More of the black-and-
white Chinese film of the figures hunting in the snow.

> LACY'S VOICE
> This last piece is optically blown
> up.

BLACK AND WHITE

Very grainy and hard to make out. Reminiscent of the
satellite blow-up footage. Barely silhouettes, they
don't look human, but they also don't look like any
recognizable animal.

> LACY'S VOICE
> This is supposedly early Chinese
> footage. The titles say it was shot
> in 1921.

> HARDAWAY'S VOICE
> It could have been faked.

> LACY'S VOICE
> It's been analyzed half a dozen
> times. Everyone says it's authentic.

The hunters have their prey and are violently
stabbing it to death.

Black screen.

The lights come on. Hardaway's loft is huge. World-
class art. A wall of books. Mementos of past extreme
adventures: cliff climbing, high-altitude ballooning,
wild river kayaking, swimming with sharks, lots and

lots of computers and monitors . . . and MATTHEW
HARDAWAY, a very rich man.

More mementos.

                    HARDAWAY
          Very cool.

A boyish midthirties, expensively dressed in a Brooks
Brothers button-down shirt, pressed jeans, and
barefoot, Hardaway hands Lacy an orange juice and
walks to the table covered with maps of the
Himalayas, large color slides of the incisor from all
angles, drawings of the man/beasts.

Lacy watches him. Hardaway checks the map of Bhutan.

                    HARDAWAY
                  (continuing)
          How many days do you see the
          expedition taking?

                    LACY
          Once we're in Bhutan, three days to
          get to Mount Chomo Lhari, then . . .
                  (smiling)
          . . . who knows.

Hardaway nods as he continues to look over Lacy's
materials.

                    HARDAWAY
          We had to trek in a week to get to a
          wilderness kayak run in Bolivia.
          Amazing to be that far away from
                  (more)

                    HARDAWAY (con't)
          civilization. I understand Bhutan's
          like that.

                         LACY
          I've been climbing in Bhutan twice
          looking for the K'ang Mi. It's like
          going back in time.

    Lacy's looking at the photographs on the wall.

                       HARDAWAY
          Mountains are really extreme. I love
          them.

    Hardaway looks at the man/beast drawings.

                       HARDAWAY
                      (continuing)
          What do you think the odds are of
          finding one of these things?

    Lacy walks over to him.

                         LACY
          Other than this footage, no one's
          ever photographed or found a K'ang
          Mi. Only footprints. There's talk of
          skins and scalps in the monasteries,
          but nothing definitive. There's a lot
          of hoaxes out there.

    Hardaway studies her.

```
            HARDAWAY
     Aren't you supposed to be hyping me
     on this?
```

Lots of new dialogue for the two main characters.

```
                LACY
     I was there in '94 and '97. We were
     underfunded. We didn't have a chance.
     I'm telling you the real deal. I've
     budgeted the expedition at a million
     dollars. That's a lot of money.

Hardaway is unfazed.

              HARDAWAY
     Let's say the expedition finds one of
     these K'ang Mi, who owns it?

Lacy studies him.

                LACY
     No one owns anyone else.

Lacy holds up the hard copy of the green dot . . .
and looks right in Hardaway's eyes.

                LACY
              (continuing)
     This expedition is going to put an
     end to all the speculation about
     K'ang Mi . . . all the hoaxes. I
     believe they're here.
```

New dialogue for Lacy. Right on point.

After a long moment . . .

> HARDAWAY
>> I'll have papers drawn up.

Lacy can't believe it. She holds out her hand.

> LACY
>> We have a deal?

> HARDAWAY
>> Deal.

He gives her a hug . . . and holds it a little too long. Lacy laughs happily as she gently pulls away from him.

A bit shorter.

> LACY
>> Thank you.

New dialogue.

> HARDAWAY
>> The publicity alone is worth more than a million.

Lacy can't stop smiling.

> LACY
>> Fantastic!

But Hardaway's not finished.

> HARDAWAY
> It has to be called the Hardaway
> Expedition.

Lacy's taken by surprise. After a beat . . .

> LACY
> OK.

> HARDAWAY
> The find has to be called Hardaway
> Man.

She looks at him for even a longer beat.

> LACY
> I'm not sure. . . .

> HARDAWAY
> (interrupting)
> And I go along on the expedition.

Hardaway holds the color slide up to the light.

> HARDAWAY
> (continuing)
> This is nonnegotiable.

Lacy looks at him in disbelief.

                                                   CUT TO:

EXT. THE HIMALAYAS - DAY

The staggering snowy crest of the Himalayas towers
over the tiny green Buddhist kingdom of Bhutan.
BUDDHIST TRANCE MUSIC plays.

EXT. THE PARO VALLEY - DAY - MUSIC CONTINUES

Fortresslike Buddhist temples, fields with herds of
yak, and the occasional ancient stone farmhouse.

In a centuries-old outbuilding, a shiny red Chinese
tractor.

EXT. PARO - DAY - MUSIC CONTINUES

A small town of low-slung ancient wooden buildings
and old people in colorful indigenous garb.

TV satellite dishes on roofs are the only objects
that distinguish it from the 1890s. Until . . .

EXT. PARO AIRPORT - DAY

The THWACKING THROB of a cargo helicopter emblazoned
with HARDAWAY EXPEDITION on the side hovers down to a
landing.

Another THROBBING helicopter drops down and lands
nearby.

The first one on the ground is already being unloaded
of high-tech plastic crates labeled HARDAWAY EXPEDI-
TION. Everything is being covered by two frantic
VIDEOGRAPHERS.

INT. PARO AIRPORT HANGAR - DAY - DOCUMENTARY VIDEO

Filled with ropes, pitons, dried-food packages, and
mountaineering and electronic equipment. More sleek
plastic cases labeled HARDAWAY EXPEDITION.

Detailed topographical maps and computer printouts
pinned to the wall. A red line is drawn from Paro to
the summit of Chomo Lhari.

SUTTON, forty, in canvas pants, a down vest, climbing
boots, and a quarter-inch buzz cut, lights a cigarette, takes a deep drag, then . . .

                    SUTTON
          (sullenly answering a question)
          Lew Sutton. I've lived in these
          hills, mostly Nepal, for the last
          fifteen, twenty years.

INT. PARO AIRPORT HANGAR - DAY

Sutton looks directly into the video camera held by
the young Videographer.

                    SUTTON
    And just to go on the record. I
    don't believe there's a K'ang Mi or
    any . . .
            (barely able to keep a straight face)
    . . . "man/beast of the Himalayas"
    up there. No big deal.

                VIDEOGRAPHER'S VOICE
    And your job is?

                    SUTTON
    Chief guide.

INT. HANGAR - DAY - VIDEO

The Videographer PANS to a laughing JAMES, twenty-
one, buffed to the extreme, taking snapshots of the
videographer shooting him, then lowering his camera.

                    JAMES
                (into camera)
    I'm James Devine. My job is to
    photograph the film crew.

Everyone LAUGHS.

                    JAMES
                (continuing)
    I'm real excited to be part of this
    whole thing. I've done Everest,
    Annapurna, Patagonia. My job is
    logistics and support, computer and
    video nerd, and I wrangle the
    satellite location system.
                (carefully)

                    JAMES (con't)
          I . . . I thought I saw something on
          Everest . . . that's why I'm here.
                    (smiling at Lacy)
          I'm looking forward to shaking that
          K'ang Mi's hand, paw, flipper, what-
          ever.

New dialogue. More into it. More color.

INT. HANGAR - DAY

James looks to his left to GABY, very athletic woman,
twenty-three, who smiles at the video camera. She's
very beautiful.

Rewritten.

                        GABY
                    (French accent)
          My name is Gabriella Probert. Gaby
          is what they call me. I was on the
          '97 Italian climb of K2. Officer
          Medicale. My English it is not so
          good, so please be patience with me.

She smiles a warm smile and looks to her left.

INT. HANGAR - DAY - VIDEO

PIRU, under five feet, indeterminate age, maybe
thirty, probably sixty, with a knowing smile,
uncomfortable with the cameras on him.

                    PIRU
          I Piru. From Bhutan. I have climb
          Chomo Lhari . . . never north face.
          No one climb north face. I have not
          seen snow demon, but . . .
                    (after a beat)
          I Piru

INT. HANGAR - DAY

Resplendent in his custom expedition-ware and
HARDAWAY EXPEDITION down jacket, Hardaway claps Piru
on the shoulder.

                    HARDAWAY
          "Snow Demon." Good name. Hi,
          everybody. I'm Hardaway.com. The
          Hardaway Group of companies. I'm
          funding the expedition . . .
                    (smiling boyishly)
          . . . Matthew.
                    (looking around)
          I can't thank you all enough for
          participating. And the reason we're
          all here . . .
                    (looking to his left)
          . . . Dr. Lacy Kendricks.

Deleted "you've probably heard of the Hardaway Group."

Everyone smiles and APPLAUDS.

Lacy blushes.

                    LACY
Thanks . . . I hope we're all
applauding as much when we come down
off the mountain.

                  HARDAWAY
We will be.

                    LACY
I'm Lacy. I've been working on this
project for over six years,
gathering data, recording anecdotal
evidence . . . believing that all of
these accounts and sightings . . .
that there must be some reality to
it. And with no support, I mean I
was out there on the edge,
alone . . .
                 (smiling)
. . . but now . . .
                 (warming)
. . . Matthew, all of you, here, on
the same page, on this expedition,
it touches me so deeply. Thank
you . . .

Much more of Lacy's journey put into dialogue. More on the nose. Much more
commercial.

She stops for a moment to gather her emotions.

                    LACY
                 (continuing)
              Thank you.

She takes a deep breath, then . . .

>   LACY
>   (continuing)
>   Okay, the bottom line on the
>   expedition is: the buck stops
>   here . . .
>   (pointing to herself)
>   . . . with me, about everything.

Lacy lets that sink in.

Sutton glances over at Hardaway, who hasn't changed
expression.

>   LACY
>   (continuing)
>   We are climbing Mount Chomo Lhari,
>   which, I'm sure you all know, is a
>   holy mountain, one of the Himalayan
>   deities.

Piru nods knowingly.

>   LACY
>   (continuing)
>   We must treat her with the utmost
>   respect. No drinking, drugs, sexual
>   activity, nothing that can be
>   considered negative or insulting in
>   any way toward the mountain.
>   Anything else, Piru?

Piru looks around at the members of the expedition
and smiles.

PIRU
Chomo Lhari forgives Westerners.

Rewritten.

Everyone looks at each other. They're nervous and
excited.

Lacy puts her hand up in the air over her head.

Gaby puts her alongside Lacy's.

James does as well.

                    HARDAWAY
        Yeah.

And he puts his hand with the others.

Finally, Sutton reluctantly joins them and they're a
team.

Deletion of page of videographers not being able to climb. Off point.

                                        CUT TO:

EXT. BHUTAN - DAY

The peaks covered with clouds.

EXT. MOUNTAIN TRAIL - DAY

Bhutanese shepherds dressed in the native <u>saros,</u>
skirtlike affairs, walk with their yak along the
well-worn paths.

The two THUMPING HARDAWAY EXPEDITION helicopters
fly low spooking the yak as they head up to Mount
Chomo Lhari.

INT. CARGO HELICOPTER - DAY

Flying low over the scruffy Himalayan wilderness. One
of the videographers shoots Piru, who looks very
trapped and unhappy in the corner. Lacy sits in the
other corner with Hardaway.

More description. Deleted first four dialogue exchanges to get into the scene
faster.

                    HARDAWAY
          I believe in you.

Lucy LAUGHS and blushes.

                    HARDAWAY
                  (continuing)
          What?

                    LACY
          The way you say it sounds like "I
          want to sleep with you."

Shorter.

Hardaway smiles.

                    HARDAWAY
          I did feel something between us at
          my place, didn't you?

Lacy nods.

Hardaway puts his hand on hers. Lacy pulls her hand
away.

>   LACY
>   It's not happening.

More direct.

>   HARDAWAY
>   I know you're not with anyone.

>   LACY
>   How do? . . .

She doesn't finish. Hardaway smiles a bad-boy smile.

>   HARDAWAY
>   I like to know who I'm in business
>   with.

>   LACY
>   Then it shouldn't come as much of a
>   surprise to you that I'm
>   saying . . .
>   (after a beat)
>   . . . thanks, but no thanks. It's
>   very flattering, but . . .
>   (laughing gently)
>   . . . I'm a little busy.

Hardaway smiles. Lacy shakes her head.

                              LACY
                          (continuing)
                  Matthew, doing anything during the
                  expedition is unprofessional,
                  counterproductive, and totally out
                  of the question. Clear enough?

Hardaway nods.

Added his action.

                              HARDAWAY
                      Absolutely.

Not believing him for a second, Lacy gets up, walks
past Sutton and James to Gaby, who's prepping the
medical supplies. James leans toward Sutton.

                              JAMES
                  She's a pretty amazing woman.

Sutton puts an unlit cigarette in his mouth.

                              SUTTON
                  Don't waste your time.

                              JAMES
                  I mean her work.

                              SUTTON
                  You would.

                              JAMES
                  Taking those manly-man pills again?

Sutton spins around to James.

                    SUTTON
        What the hell do you mean by that?

James lifts his tiny digital video camera and shoots
Sutton snarling.

New final exchange.

EXT. MOUNTAINSIDE - SUNSET

The THROBBING choppers on the ground, their
propellers still spinning.

The Videographers shoot the Westerners arguing.

                    HARDAWAY
        They can take us higher, save time.

Lacy shakes her head.

                    LACY
        Piru says the mountain doesn't like
        the noisy birds.

Hardaway looks over at the guides crouching in a
circle, passing around betel nuts and talking and
chuckling under their breath. Piru averts his eyes.

Hardaway turns back to Lacy and shields their
conversation from the camera people.

                    HARDAWAY
        These guys are like out of the
        fifteenth century. What do they know?

                              LACY
              They know the mountain.

Hardaway thinks for a moment, then shakes his head.

                            HARDAWAY
              Unbelievable.

He lifts his radio.

                            HARDAWAY
                  (continuing; into the radio)
              OK, let 'em go.

The helicopters REV UP and chopper off the mountain
leaving the hillside dotted with colorful poly tents
and the expedition.

Deleted Hardaway looking around.

It's staggering . . . and silent except for the ever-
present WIND.

Everyone looks around at the sun setting a rainbow of
colors across the valley, then look at each
other. . . .

They're alone.

The wind picks up and starts HOWLING eerily across
the face of the mountain.

EXT. MOUNTAINSIDE - NIGHT

Lights in the tents like colorful Chinese lanterns
across the face of the mountain.

```
INT. TENT - NIGHT

Lacy talks into a small tape recorder.

                    LACY
          Night one and we're on schedule.
          Perfect.
```

New scene.

Between drafts one and two, I lost eight pages. Between drafts two and three I added five pages of new characters, more dialogue, more for Lacy to do, more streamlined writing.

No one loved the script enough when I sent it out.

It sits on my shelf.

Pretty anticlimactic, huh? Yes and no. Remember, it's about the process for me, and less about selling.

Headline: "SCRIPT FOR SALE! CHEAP!!"

Fifteen

IT'S A WRAP

It's more competitive in Hollywood than it's ever been.

The screenwriting/TV writing landscape is shrinking.

Fewer scripts developed.

Fewer original scripts bought.

Fewer movies made.

Movies of the week are almost extinct.

There are more and more nonscripted reality series.

It's tough.

With fewer markets and options to sell your original screenplay, your script has to read head and shoulders above the rest.

Rewriting is your chance to elevate your script, to perfect it.

It's hard work.

It takes patience and perseverance, but it's worth it.

Rewriting takes focus.

Rewriting takes dedication.

Rewriting takes rising to the occasion to get beyond where your writing normally is.

First drafts are a suggestion, a hint of what the final scripts will ultimately become.

I hope *Rewriting Secrets for Screenwriters* has shown you the value and potential of rewriting, given you a Strategy for Rewriting—using the mini-rewrites—so you'll be able to maximize your screenplay, and shown you that rewriting is worth your time and effort.

When I finish rewriting a screenplay, I always feel wonderfully satisfied that I've brought the script closer to reaching the potential of the original idea.

Rewriting makes me feel good.

It's why I write.

Keep writing.

Tom Lazarus
http://tomlazarus.com

ACKNOWLEDGMENTS

I'd like to thank Elizabeth Beier for her guidance, Stevie Stern Lazarus for her round-the-clock support, Alison Lazarus for her goodwill, the UCLA Extension Writing Program for their courage to employ a slightly out-of-the-box instructor, the very generous Scott Frank, Laura Simmons for her impeccable research, my circle of supportive longtime friends, and, last but not least, all the readers of *Secrets of Film Writing,* who have encouraged me, as I have encouraged them, to keep writing.

When you start a rewrite, cut this out and tape it in a conspicuous place where you work.

Cut here---

A STRATEGY FOR REWRITING

- Gain new perspective

- Prioritize big scenes

- Track transitions

- Plot corrections

- Make sure every scene moves the story forward

- Dialogue must sound good

- Subtext, subtext, subtext

The more you rewrite, the better your script will be.